ISLE OF MAN

GUIDE 2024

Expert Guide to The Best Best Destinations, Timeless Beauty, Culture, Hidden Gems and has Maps and 5-day Itinerary Appropriate For First Time Visitors.

GW01312762

GLOBAL DESTINATIONS
CARAWAY TRAVELS

Richard Caraway

Disclaimer.

The information contained in this book is for general information purposes only. The author and publisher have made every effort to ensure the accuracy of the information provided, but make no guarantees or warranties of any kind, express or implied, about the completeness, accuracy, reliability, suitability, or availability of the information and resources contained herein.

This book is intended to provide helpful and informative content to readers, but it should not be relied upon as a substitute for professional advice. The author and publisher are not responsible for any errors or omissions, or for the results obtained from the use of this information.

Readers are advised to verify any information contained in this book with other reliable sources and to exercise their own judgment when planning and booking travel arrangements. The author and publisher shall not be liable for any losses, injuries, or damages from the display or use of this information.

Flag of the Isle of Man - Manx Flag

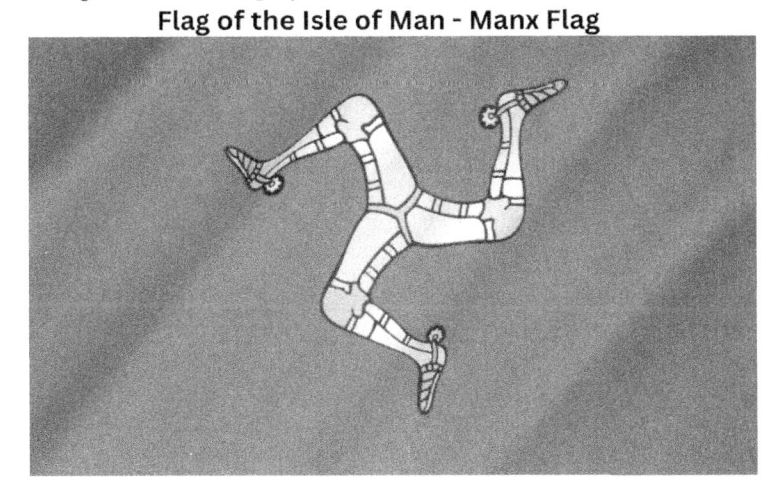

Contents

CHAPTER 1.

INTRODUCTION TO THE ISLE OF MAN

Welcome to the Isle of Man.

If you were to pose a word association game to a group of friends about the Isle of Man, chances are the responses would paint a picture of a mysterious, timeless land - phrases like "rugged beauty," "Celtic heritage," and "unspoiled wonder" might spring forth. And rightfully so, for this enchanting island situated between the United Kingdom and Ireland is a realm unto itself, a place that seems to exist in a realm outside the constraints of time.

As you step onto this enchanting isle, you'll be instantly captivated by its timeless charm and unwavering spirit. The Isle of

Man is a place where the past and present seamlessly intertwine, creating a tapestry of experiences that will leave a lasting impression on all who visit.

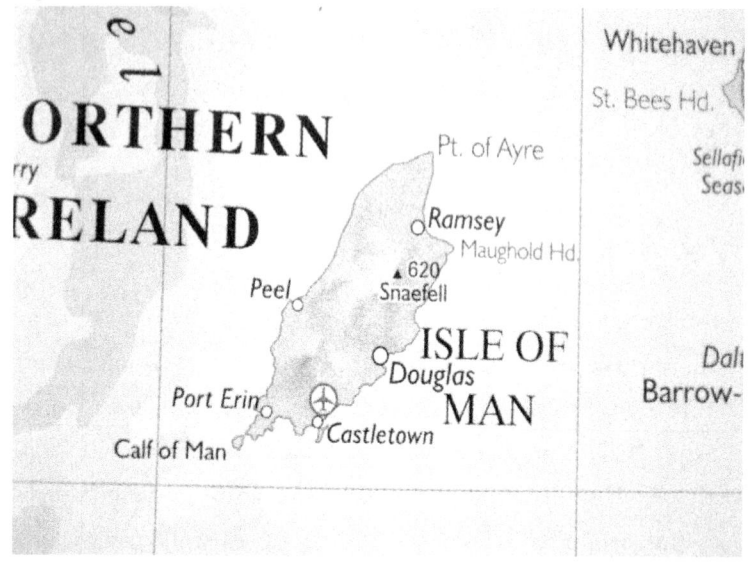

The island's diverse landscapes will impress you from the moment you arrive. Rugged coastal cliffs give way to lush glens, while rolling hills and tranquil glens provide a peaceful escape from the outside world. The island's distinctive geological formations, such as the iconic Cregneash Village and the awe-inspiring Laxey Wheel, reflect the island's rich history and the ingenuity of its people.

The Isle of Man, on the other hand, is a cultural and historical center in addition to its natural wonders. The island's rich Celtic heritage is reflected in its ancient monuments, including Tynwald Hill, where the island's parliament has met for over a millennium. Douglas, the island's capital, is a vibrant and cosmopolitan city with a thriving arts, museum, and culinary scene.

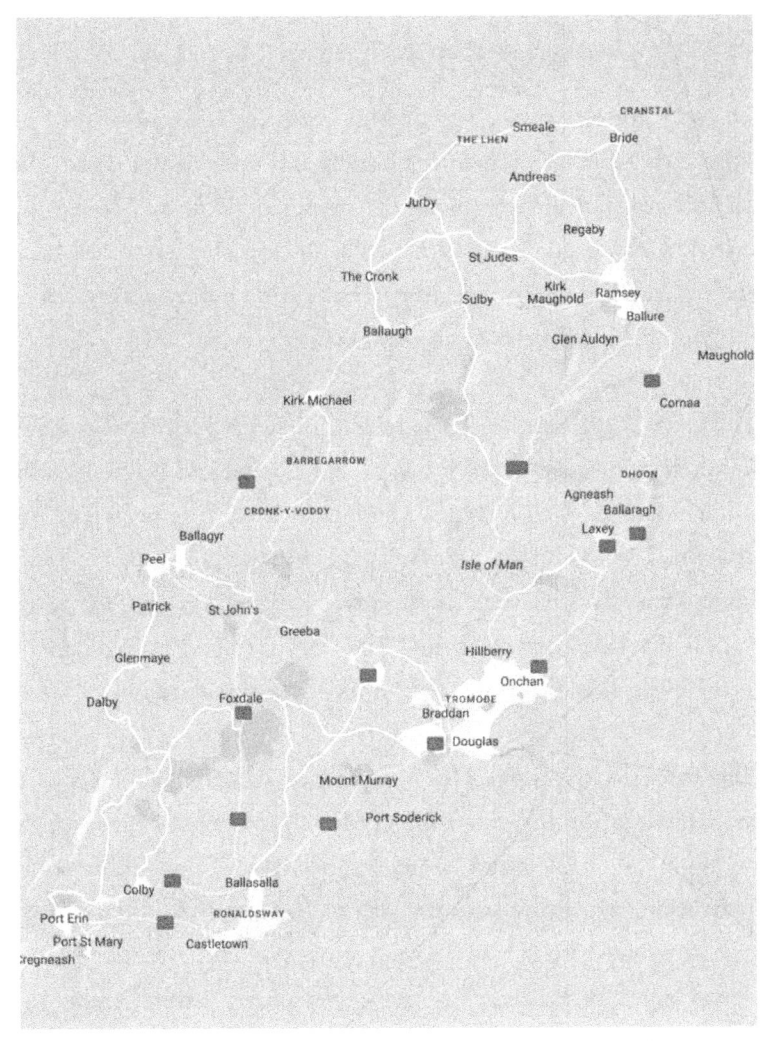

Whether you're looking for outdoor adventures, a fascinating history, or vibrant cultural offerings, the Isle of Man will captivate and delight. So get ready to embark on an unforgettable journey to this enchanting island, where the past and present collide to create a truly unforgettable experience.

History and Culture of the Island

To truly appreciate the Isle of Man, one must first dive into its rich and captivating history, which has indelibly shaped the island's cultural identity over the centuries. This self-governing British Crown dependency boasts a lineage that stretches back millennia, with evidence of human habitation dating as far back as the Mesolithic period around 6500 BC.

The Isle of Man's strategic location in the Irish Sea has long made it a prized possession, and it has been occupied and influenced by a succession of Celtic, Norse, and British powers over its long history. The island's Celtic heritage is especially visible, with ancient monuments such as the Megalithic tombs at Cashtal yn Ard, which date back to around 3000 BC and serve as a testament to the ingenuity and spirituality of its early inhabitants.

The Tynwald, the Isle of Man's ancient parliament that has met in the same location for over a millennium, is one of the most iconic symbols of the island's Celtic heritage. This remarkable institution, which predates the British Parliament and dates back at least to the 10th century AD, is a living example of the island's unwavering dedication to self-government and democratic principles.

The influence of Norse culture on the Isle of Man is also deeply ingrained, as Viking raiders established a stronghold there in the ninth century AD. This is demonstrated by the prevalence of Norse place names, the iconic Manx cat breed with its distinctive tailless appearance, and the island's extensive folklore traditions.

Over the centuries, the Isle of Man's allegiances shifted between the British Crown and the Kingdom of Scotland, with the island eventually becoming a Crown dependency in the 14th century. The Isle of Man's unique political status has allowed it to maintain some autonomy while still benefiting from its close ties to the UK.

Today, the Isle of Man's fascinating history pervades every aspect of its cultural fabric. From the traditional Manx language, which is a mix of Gaelic and English and has been spoken on the island since the 5th century AD, to the island's vibrant festivals and customs, the past is ever-present, shaping both locals' and visitors' experiences.

Whether you're exploring the ancient sites dotting the island's landscape, immersing yourself in the rich tapestry of Manx folklore, or simply soaking up the unique atmosphere that pervades every corner of this enchanting isle, you'll be struck by the Isle of Man's enduring legacy.

Geography and Natural Landscapes

Situated between the islands of Great Britain and Ireland in the heart of the Irish Sea, the Isle of Man boasts a unique and captivating geography that has profoundly shaped its cultural and natural heritage. Spanning just 221 square miles, this self-governing British Crown dependency is a veritable treasure trove of diverse and stunning landscapes.

The central mountain range runs through the island and is dominated by the impressive summit of Snaefell, which rises to 2,036 feet (620 meters). This rugged, heather-clad massif is the highest point on the Isle of Man, providing breathtaking views of the island and surrounding seas. A series of smaller upland areas surround the central mountains, including the stunning Sloc Hills and the dramatic Calf of Man cliffs.

Ancient glacial activity created a network of deep glens, or "gullies," that cut through the island's interior. These verdant, winding valleys, such as the famous Glen Darragh and Gleinn Chass, are home to a diverse range of native flora and fauna, including the elusive Manx shearwater, a seabird that nests in burrows along the island's rocky coastline.

The Isle of Man's coastline is equally captivating, with a wide variety of geological formations and ecosystems. The land on the island's eastern and northern shores gives way to dramatic sea cliffs, punctuated by hidden coves, sea caves, and natural arches carved out by the relentless pounding of the Irish Sea. The island's western and southern coasts, on the other hand, feature wide sandy beaches and dunes, such as the well-known Peel Beach and the sprawling Langness Peninsula.

Offshore, the Isle of Man is home to a number of smaller islets and rock formations, the most notable of which is the Calf of Man, a small island designated as a nature reserve and an important seabird breeding ground. The island's coastal waters are also teeming with marine life, with a wide variety of fish, cetaceans, and other aquatic species flourishing in the nutrient-rich Irish Sea.

A complex and ancient geological history serves as the foundation for the Isle of Man's diverse and breathtaking landscapes. The island's bedrock is primarily made up of Manx Slate, a metamorphic rock from the Precambrian era, as well as Carboniferous limestone and sandstone. These diverse geological strata have been sculpted and shaped over millennia by glacial activity, weathering, and the constant force of the surrounding seas.

Whether you're exploring the rugged uplands, meandering through the enchanting glens, or admiring the dramatic coastline, the Isle of Man's captivating geography and natural landscapes will leave an indelible impression. This small but surprisingly diverse island is a true natural wonder, allowing visitors to immerse themselves in a world of breathtaking beauty and ecological richness.

Getting to the Isle of Man

Reaching the enchanting Isle of Man can be a delightful and seamless experience, thanks to the island's well-connected transportation infrastructure and its convenient location between Great Britain and Ireland. Whether you're planning a day trip, a weekend getaway, or an extended stay, there are several options to consider when making your travel arrangements.

By Air:

The Isle of Man is served by the Isle of Man Airport (IOM), located just a few miles outside the capital city of Douglas. This modern airport handles a range of domestic and international flights, with regular scheduled services from various airports in the United Kingdom, including London, Manchester, Liverpool, and Birmingham. Many major airlines, such as British Airways, EasyJet, and Loganair, offer direct flights to the Isle of Man, making it easily accessible from most parts of the UK.

When booking your flights, keep in mind that the Isle of Man Airport is a small facility, so arrive well in advance of your scheduled departure time to ensure efficient check-in and security procedures. Furthermore, the airport's remote location necessitates the use of ground transportation, such as taxis or car rentals, to reach your destination on the island.

By Sea:

For those looking for a more scenic and leisurely journey, the Isle of Man is also accessible by sea. The Isle of Man is served by several ferry services, which connect it to various ports in the United Kingdom and Ireland.

The most popular ferry route is from the English port of Liverpool, which takes approximately 2.5 hours. This service is run by the Isle of Man Steam Packet Company, the island's primary ferry operator. Alternatively, you can travel to the Isle of Man from the Irish ports of Dublin and Belfast, which take approximately 3-4 hours.

When planning your ferry trip, make sure to check the schedule and book your tickets ahead of time, especially during peak travel seasons or special events. Furthermore, if you're bringing a vehicle, make sure to reserve your spot early, as ferry capacity for cars is limited.

Once you've arrived on the island, you'll find an efficient public transportation network that includes buses, trains, and the iconic Isle of Man Steam Railway, which offers a delightful and nostalgic way to explore the island's picturesque countryside and coastline.

Regardless of your mode of transportation, the journey to the Isle of Man is part of the adventure, providing breathtaking views and insight into the island's rich maritime history. With careful planning and an adventurous spirit, you're sure to have an unforgettable trip to this captivating and unique destination.

CHAPTER 2.

DOUGLAS - THE VIBRANT CAPITAL

Exploring the Historic Harbor Front

At the heart of the Isle of Man's captivating capital city of Douglas lies the historic harbor front, a bustling and charming area that offers visitors a glimpse into the island's rich maritime heritage and vibrant cultural life. As you stroll along the picturesque promenade, you'll be enchanted by the picturesque Victorian architecture, the lively waterfront activities, and the stunning views across the sparkling waters of the Irish Sea.

One of the must-see attractions along the harborfront is Douglas Harbor, a thriving commercial and recreational hub that has played an important role in the island's history. Wander along the quaysides, admiring the impressive fleet of fishing boats, ferries, and private yachts that call this harbor home. Visit the historic Tower of Refuge, a one-of-a-kind stone structure that once housed shipwrecked sailors, and take in the breathtaking views of the harbor and surrounding headlands.

As you explore the harbor, keep an eye out for the iconic Isle of Man Steam Packet Company, the island's main ferry operator. This historic company has been providing ferry services to and from the Isle of Man for over 180 years, and you may be lucky enough to see one of their impressive passenger ferries arrive or depart.

No trip to the Douglas Harbor front would be complete without sampling the local seafood. Make your way to one of the many charming waterfront restaurants and cafes to sample fresh-caught lobster, crab, and Manx kippers, a traditional smoked herring that has been a staple of the island's cuisine for centuries. Enjoy your meal with a refreshing pint of local Manx ale or a glass of crisp white wine while taking in the vibrant atmosphere of this bustling harbor community.

If you prefer a more active exploration of the harbor, consider taking a scenic boat tour or renting a kayak or paddleboard to explore the sheltered waters at your leisure. These unique vantage points provide stunning views of the harbor's historic architecture, the Manx coastline, and the surrounding hills.

As the sun sets, the harbor front takes on a magical quality, with historic buildings and landmarks bathed in a warm, golden light. This is the ideal time to stroll along the promenade, eat some local ice cream, and watch as both island residents and visitors gather to enjoy the tranquil beauty of the harbor and the breathtaking natural landscapes that surround it.

Whether you're drawn to the historic charm, culinary delights, or opportunities for outdoor adventure, the Douglas Harbor front is a must-see destination that will leave an indelible impression on everyone who visits. So, celebrate the island's maritime heritage, savor the local flavors, and immerse yourself in the vibrant spirit of this captivating capital city.

Top Attractions in Douglas

As the vibrant capital and largest city of the Isle of Man, Douglas offers a wealth of captivating attractions that showcase the island's rich history, cultural heritage, and natural beauty. From iconic landmarks to breathtaking vantage points, there is something to enchant every visitor. Let's explore the top attractions in Douglas and uncover the unique experiences they offer.

The Manx Museum:
Located in the heart of Douglas, the Manx Museum is a true treasure trove of the island's history and culture. This impressive institution houses an extensive collection of artifacts, exhibits, and interactive displays that transport visitors through the Isle of Man's captivating past, from its ancient Celtic roots to its rich maritime heritage. Visitors can learn about the island's geological formation, the intricate customs and traditions of the Manx people, and the breathtaking collection of Manx art and literature. The museum's knowledgeable staff are available to give insightful guided tours and answer any questions, making it an enriching and educational experience for all. The best time to visit is in the morning or early afternoon, when the museum is less crowded and you can fully immerse yourself in the exhibits at your own pace.

The Laxey Wheel:
Just outside of Douglas, visit the charming village of Laxey, home to the iconic Laxey Wheel, also known as "Lady Isabella." This magnificent water wheel, the largest of its kind in the world, exemplifies the island's industrial history and ingenuity in harnessing renewable energy sources. Visitors can admire the sheer

size and engineering prowess of this 72.5-foot-wide wheel, which was once used to pump water from nearby mines. Take the time to visit the nearby Laxey Woollen Mills, where you can see the traditional process of Manx textile production and buy unique local crafts. The best time to visit the Laxey Wheel is during the warmer months, when the site is fully operational and the surrounding countryside is most beautiful.

The Snaefell Mountain Railway

For a truly breathtaking experience, take a ride on the historic Snaefell Mountain Railway, which transports passengers to the top of the island's highest peak, Snaefell Mountain. This charming narrow-gauge railway, dating back to the late nineteenth century, provides panoramic views of the Manx countryside, the Irish Sea, and, on a clear day, the coasts of England, Ireland, Scotland, and Wales. Upon arrival at the summit, visitors can take in the breathtaking views, explore the visitor center, and even enjoy a cup of tea at the Snaefell Summit Café. The best time to ride the Snaefell Mountain Railway is during the summer months, when the weather is pleasant and visibility is excellent, allowing for unobstructed views of the breathtaking scenery.

Great Laxey Mine Railway:

The Great Laxey Mine Railway offers a unique and immersive glimpse into the island's industrial past. This restored mining railway system transports visitors through the once-thriving lead and zinc mines, providing an intriguing glimpse into the harsh realities of nineteenth-century mining operations. Ride the narrow-gauge railway deep underground, explore the intricate network of tunnels and shafts, and learn about the innovative engineering solutions that kept this vital industry running. The best time to visit is during the summer, when the mine's operating hours are extended and the temperature underground is a welcome relief from the heat on the surface.

These are just a few of the fascinating attractions Douglas and the surrounding area have to offer. Whether you're interested in history, engineering, or simply taking in the natural beauty of the

Isle of Man, these top attractions will leave a lasting impression and inspire you to explore the island's many wonders.

Dining and Nightlife in Douglas

Located along the picturesque harbor front, the vibrant city of Douglas offers an enticing array of dining and nightlife options that showcase the best of Manx cuisine and culture. As a long-time visitor to the Isle of Man, I'm excited to share my insider recommendations to help you make the most of your culinary and social experiences in this captivating capital.

Dining in Douglas

The Courthouse: Located in the heart of Douglas' historic city center, The Courthouse is a hidden gem for those seeking a refined and sophisticated dining experience. This acclaimed restaurant, housed in a beautifully restored 19th-century courthouse, serves a menu that highlights the island's local bounty, including fresh-caught seafood and premium Manx beef. Try their signature Manx kippers and Queenies (Manx queen scallops), which are local delicacies perfected over generations. The Courthouse's elegant decor, attentive service, and breathtaking views of the harbor make it ideal for a celebratory meal or a romantic date night.

Crust: For a more casual but equally enjoyable dining experience, visit Crust, a popular pizzeria located just a short walk from the harbor. Crust serves a tantalizing selection of wood-fired Neapolitan-style pizzas that highlight the island's exceptional local produce and artisanal techniques. From the classic Margherita to the inventive Manx Kipper pizza, every slice demonstrates the chefs' dedication to quality and creativity. Pair your pizza with a refreshing local craft beer or a glass of crisp white wine, and enjoy the lively atmosphere and breathtaking views of the harbor.

Mona's: No visit to Douglas is complete without sampling the authentic flavors of traditional Manx cuisine, and Mona's is the ideal place to do so. This charming family-run restaurant, just a stone's throw from the promenade, serves a menu that highlights the island's diverse culinary heritage. Enjoy hearty dishes such as Manx lamb stew, traditional Manx kippers, and the popular Lough Calf (Manx beef), all made with time-honored recipes and locally sourced ingredients. The cozy, welcoming atmosphere and friendly service make Mona's a must-see for anyone looking for a true taste of the Isle of Man.

The Sidings: Housed in a beautifully restored Victorian railway station, The Sidings is a one-of-a-kind dining experience that blends industrial chic with modern culinary flair. The menu is an enticing blend of traditional British cuisine and innovative international influences, highlighting the island's abundant seafood and produce. Fresh crab cakes, pan-seared Manx scallops, and decadent sticky toffee pudding are among the standout dishes. Pair your meal with a wine selection from their extensive list, or try one of the island's famous local beers on tap. The Sidings' beautiful setting and impeccable service make it an excellent choice for a special occasion or memorable dining experience.

The Claremont: For a truly luxurious dining experience, reserve a table at The Claremont, a Michelin-starred restaurant housed in the iconic Claremont Hotel. The Claremont, led by renowned chef Kevin Charters, serves a menu that combines contemporary techniques with traditional Manx flavors. Savor exquisitely presented dishes made with the finest local ingredients, such as succulent Manx lamb, delicate Peel crab, and decadent Manx-produced chocolate. The Claremont's intimate setting, attentive service, and impeccable wine pairing recommendations make it a culinary treasure on the Isle of Man.

Nightlife in Douglas

The Britannia: For a lively and authentic Manx nightlife experience, head to The Britannia, a traditional pub located just a short walk from the harbor. This beloved local institution has been serving up pints of Manx-brewed ale and hosting lively music sessions for over a century. Step inside and you'll be greeted by the warm, convivial atmosphere and the sound of live traditional Manx music, ranging from folk ballads to rousing fiddle tunes. The Britannia is a hub for the island's vibrant music scene, and catching a performance here is a must for any visitor looking to immerse themselves in the island's cultural heritage.

The Velvet Coaster: If you're looking for a more modern and eclectic nightlife experience, head to The Velvet Coaster, a stylish cocktail bar and nightclub on the promenade. This sleek and sophisticated establishment serves an impressive menu of expertly crafted cocktails, many of which incorporate locally sourced ingredients and Manx-distilled spirits. As the night progresses, the venue transforms into a lively dance floor, with a DJ spinning a diverse mix of contemporary music to keep you dancing all night. The Velvet Coaster's chic decor and breathtaking views of the harbor make it a popular spot for both locals and visitors.

The Archibald Knox: For a more relaxed and intimate nightlife experience, stop by The Archibald Knox, a cozy whisky and gin bar named after the renowned Manx designer. This charming establishment serves a wide range of premium spirits, with an emphasis on locally produced Manx whisky and gin. Settle into one of the plush leather armchairs, sip an expertly mixed cocktail, and soak up the refined, sophisticated atmosphere. The Archibald Knox also hosts regular live music performances, showcasing the island's talented local musicians and providing the ideal setting for a relaxing evening of conversation and indulgence.

The Villa Marina: No Douglas nightlife guide would be complete without mentioning the iconic Villa Marina, a multi-purpose entertainment complex that has served as the cultural hub of the city for over a century. This grand, neoclassical structure houses a number of venues, including a concert hall, a theater, and a ballroom, making it a hotspot for live music, comedy, and dance shows. Throughout the year, the Villa Marina hosts a diverse range of events, from classical orchestral concerts to contemporary rock shows, catering to a wide range of tastes and interests. Whether you're seeing a show, attending a special event, or simply exploring the building's stunning architecture, a visit to the Villa Marina is a must for any visitor to Douglas.

The Manx Arms: For a more traditional and lively pub experience, head to The Manx Arms, a local favorite located near the harbor. This authentic Manx pub serves as a gathering place for the island's residents, with a welcoming atmosphere and a selection of locally brewed ales and lagers. In the evenings, The

Manx Arms frequently hosts live music performances, which range from traditional Manx folk sessions to modern indie and rock acts. It's the ideal place to mingle with locals, sample the island's renowned brewing scene, and soak up the vibrant, welcoming atmosphere that defines Manx nightlife.

Whether you're looking for a refined dining experience, a lively night of music and dancing, or a cozy, intimate gathering, Douglas has a variety of options to suit your taste and preferences. Exploring these recommended dining and nightlife establishments will allow you to not only enjoy the exceptional flavors and experiences that the Isle of Man has to offer, but also gain a better understanding of the island's rich cultural heritage and warm, welcoming community.

Shopping in the Island's Capital

As the commercial heart of the Isle of Man, the city of Douglas offers a captivating shopping experience that seamlessly blends the island's rich heritage with contemporary flair. Whether you're in pursuit of authentic Manx-made crafts, gourmet local delicacies, or the latest fashion trends, this seaside capital promises to delight and surprise the discerning shopper at every turn.

Begin your shopping adventure at the Manx Emporium, a charming department store situated on the picturesque Douglas Promenade. Stepping inside this veritable treasure trove, you'll be greeted by an impressive collection of locally produced arts, crafts, textiles, and specialty food items that celebrate the island's cultural heritage. Explore the shelves and you'll discover intricate lace work, cozy Manx-knit sweaters, and traditional tartan accessories, all imbued with the captivating island's distinct character and traditions. The knowledgeable staff is eager to share the stories behind these one-of-a-kind products, making the Manx Emporium an excellent place to not only find authentic Manx souvenirs, but also to gain a better understanding of the island's creative spirit. Make sure to ask about their frequent sales and promotions, which can provide excellent value for money and allow you to indulge in some retail therapy without breaking the bank.

For a more immersive shopping experience, visit the Strand Street area, Douglas' vibrant commercial district. This bustling pedestrian-friendly district is lined with an eclectic mix of independent boutiques, specialty shops, and high-street favorites, providing a delightful blend of the familiar and the unusual. Strolling down the charming cobblestone streets, you'll come across hidden gems like The Parachute Store, a wonderfully quirky outdoor gear and adventure-inspired souvenir shop, and the Manannan's Isle Antiques Centre, a veritable treasure trove of Manx collectibles and vintage curios. To make the most of your time in this enthralling shopping district, I recommend arriving early in the morning, when the streets are quieter and you can better navigate the diverse array of offerings without being crowded.

No trip to Douglas would be complete without a stop at the Isle of Man Farmers' Market, which is held every Saturday morning in the heart of the city. This vibrant open-air market brings together the island's best food producers, allowing you to sample a wide range of local delicacies and artisanal goods. Browse the stalls and you'll find everything from award-winning Manx cheeses and preserves to freshly caught seafood and seasonal produce, all of which make excellent edible souvenirs or gifts. Arrive early to get the best selection and enjoy the lively atmosphere before the crowds arrive. As an added bonus, many of the vendors provide generous samples, allowing you to sample the exceptional flavors of the Isle of Man before making a purchase.

For a more modern and comprehensive shopping experience, visit The Parade Shopping Center, the island's premier indoor mall.

This sleek complex, just a short walk from the harbor, is home to a diverse range of high-street fashion retailers, specialty stores, and dining options. Browse the latest trends at Debenhams and H&M, or visit one of the unique boutiques that sell Manx-designed clothing and accessories. Visit the Shoppers Rewards Lounge to sign up for exclusive discounts and offers to maximize your shopping experience. The Parade Shopping Centre is an excellent one-stop shop for all of your retail needs, thanks to its convenient location, ample parking, and wide range of amenities.

If you're looking for truly unique and one-of-a-kind souvenirs, head to Harbour Lights, a delightful emporium located just steps from the harbor. This charming store specializes in nautical-themed gifts and home decor, with an impressive selection of handcrafted ship models, vintage sailing maps, and locally sourced seaglass jewelry. The friendly staff is enthusiastic about the island's seafaring heritage and eager to share their knowledge, making Harbour Lights an ideal location for discovering exceptional treasures and learning more about the Isle of Man's rich maritime culture.

As you explore Douglas' diverse shopping options, keep an eye out for special promotions, discounts, and loyalty programs to help you maximize your savings. Many stores, especially local boutiques and specialty shops, may provide discounts for cash payments or customers who present a valid Isle of Man resident card. Furthermore, inquire about any seasonal sales or clearance events, as these can provide excellent opportunities to get great deals on a variety of products.

Whether you want to add to your collection of Manx-made crafts, stock up on gourmet local delicacies, or simply indulge in some retail therapy, the vibrant capital of Douglas is sure to delight and captivate the discerning shopper. So, embrace your inner explorer and let the charming streets of this seaside city lead you on an unforgettable shopping adventure that showcases the best of the Isle of Man.

CHAPTER 3.

DISCOVERING THE SCENIC COASTAL DRIVES

The Coastal Road to Laxey and Ramsey

As you depart the vibrant capital of Douglas and set out along the island's eastern coastline, you'll be treated to a breathtaking panorama that showcases the Isle of Man's natural splendor in all its glory. Winding your way north on the Coastal Road, you'll be mesmerized by the dramatic cliffs, secluded coves, and sweeping vistas that unfold before you, offering a captivating introduction to the island's rugged beauty.

The first stop on your scenic coastal journey is the charming village of Laxey, which is about 8 miles north of Douglas. As you approach Laxey, you'll be captivated by the iconic Laxey Wheel, a Victorian-era waterwheel standing 72.5 feet (22 meters) tall. This incredible engineering feat, known as "Lady Isabella," was once the world's largest working waterwheel and is still a testament to the island's rich industrial heritage. Make sure to visit the Laxey Wheel exhibition and visitor center, which delves into the history and mechanics of this incredible structure, providing an intriguing glimpse into the island's past.

Laxey Harbor

Continue north from Laxey along the scenic Coastal Road, where you'll be treated to a series of breathtaking views of the Irish Sea's raw power and natural splendor. Keep an eye out for the dramatic cliffs of the Gob ny Rona headland, where the road runs dangerously close to the churning waters below. For the more daring traveler, consider taking one of the coastal walking trails that follow the rugged shoreline, providing unparalleled opportunities to immerse yourself in the island's breathtaking natural landscapes.

As you approach Ramsey, the northernmost point of your coastal adventure, you'll be greeted by a picturesque harbor and a charming town center with a delightful seaside atmosphere. Spend some time strolling along the Ramsey Promenade, admiring the town's elegant Victorian-era architecture, browsing the local shops and galleries, and perhaps indulging in a freshly caught seafood lunch or traditional Manx ice cream.

Consider taking a short detour to the Milntown Estate, a beautifully preserved country house and gardens located just a few miles outside Ramsey. Wander the estate's meticulously manicured grounds, explore the historic manor house, and learn about the fascinating history of this significant Manx landmark. Be sure to ask about any special events or exhibitions that may be taking place during your visit, as the Milntown Estate is a hub for cultural activities and community celebrations.

As you reluctantly leave Ramsey and begin your return journey to Douglas, take a moment to appreciate the breathtaking views and sense of tranquillity that pervade this coastal stretch of the island. Whether you choose to explore the quaint villages, go on a coastal hike, or simply enjoy the scenic drive, this captivating journey along the Coastal Road will leave a lasting impression on your memories of the Isle of Man.

A few tips to enhance your coastal driving experience:
1. Be sure to fill up your tank before setting out, as gas stations can be few and far between along the Coastal Road.
2. Keep a keen eye out for local wildlife, such as seabirds, seals, and even the occasional basking shark or dolphin.
3. Dress in layers and bring along a windbreaker, as the coastal winds can be quite brisk, even on a sunny day.
4. Pack a picnic lunch or snacks to enjoy at one of the many scenic pullouts along the way.
5. Consider stopping at one of the island's charming coastal villages, such as Laxey or Ramsey, to explore the local shops, pubs, and eateries.

With its dramatic cliffs, secluded coves, and charming seaside towns, the Coastal Road from Douglas to Laxey and Ramsey offers a truly captivating and unforgettable experience for the discerning traveler to the Isle of Man. So, hop in your car, take a deep breath of the salty sea air, and let this scenic coastal journey sweep you away to a realm of natural wonder and Manx hospitality.

Panoramic Views from the Mountain Road

Winding its way through the island's rugged central spine, the aptly named Mountain Road offers travelers an unparalleled opportunity to immerse themselves in the Isle of Man's extraordinary natural splendor. Climbing steadily from the coast, this captivating route treats visitors to a mesmerizing succession of panoramic viewpoints that showcase the island's dramatic topography in all its glory.

The Sloc Viewpoint, located about 9 miles south of Ramsey, is one of the most breathtaking vantage points on the journey. Here, you'll be treated to a simply breathtaking 360-degree panorama that includes the island's craggy central peaks, the shimmering waters of the Irish Sea, and, on a clear day, the distant outlines of Cumbrian fells across the water. Take a moment to appreciate the tranquility of this sublime setting, and keep your camera ready to capture the magnificent landscapes that unfold before you.

Continuing your journey, the Mountain Road will take you through the island's central uplands, which are marked by rugged moorlands, glacial valleys, and the towering peaks of Snaefell and the Beinn y Phott range. At the Mountain Road's summit, you'll find the Bungalow Pass, which, at 1,824 feet (556 meters), provides another breathtaking panoramic view. From this high vantage point, you'll be treated to sweeping views of the island's dramatic interior, including the wild, windswept landscapes of the Manx uplands.

For the more daring traveler, the Mountain Road connects to a network of hiking trails that lead deep into the island's remote interior. Consider taking a leisurely stroll along the Millennium Way, a long-distance footpath that runs through the Manx uplands, providing numerous opportunities to immerse yourself in the island's rugged natural beauty and rich cultural heritage.

As you make your way back towards the coast, keep an eye out for the island's diverse wildlife, including the iconic Manx shearwater, which can frequently be seen soaring gracefully above the surrounding moorlands. Keep an eye out for the elusive and enigmatic Manx cabbage, a rare endemic plant that clings tenaciously to the island's exposed cliff faces and rocky outcroppings.

Whether you choose to simply enjoy the breathtaking scenic drive or explore one of the Mountain Road's many hiking trails, this captivating journey through the heart of the Isle of Man will leave an indelible impression. So embrace the island's wild and untamed spirit, and allow the panoramic views of the Mountain Road to inspire and captivate you.

A few tips to enhance your Mountain Road experience:
1. Be sure to fill up your tank before setting out, as gas stations can be scarce along this remote stretch of road.
2. Dress in layers and bring along a warm jacket, as the mountain temperatures can be considerably cooler than the coastal regions.
3. Pack a picnic lunch or snacks to enjoy at one of the many scenic pullouts along the way.
4. Consider stopping at the Snaefell Summit, accessible via the Snaefell Mountain Railway, for breathtaking 360-degree views of the island.
5. Keep a keen eye out for the island's diverse array of wildlife, including wild Manx loghtan sheep, Peregrine falcons, and the elusive Manx cabbage.

Seaside Towns and Villages along the Coast

Enchanting seaside towns and villages dotting the rugged shoreline of the Isle of Man will enchant you as you travel along its captivating coastal roads. These alluring locations showcase the island's rich cultural legacy, breathtaking natural settings, and friendly people, providing a distinctive window into the Manx way of life.

Port Erin, a picturesque seaside haven on the island's southwestern tip, is one of the most enjoyable coastal villages to visit. Port Erin, nestled in a sheltered bay, exudes the quintessential seaside ambiance, with its elegant Victorian-era promenade, pristine sandy beaches, and a charming harbor that serves as a hub for local fishing and boating activities. Wander the quaint streets, and you'll come across a plethora of independent shops, galleries, and restaurants that celebrate the island's artisanal crafts and culinary heritage. Visit the Nautical Museum for a fascinating look at the village's maritime history, or take a scenic coastal walk along the spectacular Burrow and Bay Trail, which provides hikers with breathtaking views of the Calf of Man and the Irish Sea.

Port Erin, Isle of Man

Continue your coastal journey northward, and you'll come across the picturesque village of Port St. Mary, a charming community known for its picturesque harbor, breathtaking coastal landscapes, and diverse cultural offerings. Stroll along the harbor's edge and you'll come across a delightful selection of seafood restaurants, traditional pubs, and boutique shops specializing in Manx-made crafts and artisanal products. For a more in-depth look at the village's history, visit the Cregneash Folk Museum, which showcases the island's traditional way of life through a collection of lovingly restored historic buildings and exhibits. Nature lovers will also appreciate the village's proximity to the Chickens Nature Reserve, a designated Area of Special Scientific Interest with a diverse range of seabirds, wildflowers, and other fascinating flora and fauna.

As you continue north along the island's eastern coastline, you will arrive in the charming town of Castletown, the former capital of the Isle of Man and a destination that seamlessly blends its rich historical heritage with a vibrant modern energy. The impressive

Castletown Castle, located in the heart of town, is a remarkably well-preserved medieval fortress that serves as a testament to the island's strategic importance over the centuries. Explore the castle's grand halls, subterranean passages, and imposing curtain walls, and don't miss the nearby House of Manannan, an interactive museum dedicated to the island's Celtic, Viking, and maritime heritage. Beyond the castle, you'll find a charming town center lined with Georgian-era buildings, independent shops, and traditional Manx pubs, each providing a warm welcome and insight into the island's distinct culture.

Peel, located further north, is a picturesque fishing port and the center of the island's seafaring traditions. Wander the lively harbor and you'll come across a bustling fish market where you can buy the day's fresh catch or eat a delicious seafood lunch at one of the local restaurants. Make sure to visit Peel Castle, an impressive medieval fortress perched atop a rocky headland with breathtaking views of the surrounding coastline and the Irish Sea. Consider taking a short boat trip to the Calf of Man, a designated national nature reserve where you can see a variety of seabirds, seals, and other marine life.

As you continue your coastal exploration, the charming town of Ramsey awaits, offering a delightful blend of seaside charm and modern conveniences. Stroll along the Ramsey Promenade to admire the town's elegant Victorian-era architecture, browse the local shops and galleries, and maybe even stop for a freshly caught seafood lunch or a traditional Manx ice cream. For a truly memorable experience, take a short detour to the Milntown Estate, a beautifully preserved country house and gardens located just a few miles outside of Ramsey, where you can learn about this significant Manx landmark.

Finally, no discussion of the Isle of Man's coastal towns and villages is complete without mentioning Douglas, the island's vibrant capital and commercial and cultural hub. Explore the picturesque Douglas Promenade, stroll through the Strand Street district's eclectic mix of independent boutiques and high-street favorites, or learn about the island's history at the Manx Museum. For a truly one-of-a-kind shopping experience, stop by the Manx Emporium, a charming department store with a breathtaking selection of locally produced arts, crafts, and specialty foods.

As you travel along the Isle of Man's stunning coastline, you'll be enchanted by the island's diverse collection of seaside towns and villages, each offering a unique perspective on the Manx way of life. Whether you want to immerse yourself in the island's rich history, indulge in its exceptional culinary offerings, or simply bask in the natural splendor of its rugged shoreline, these captivating coastal destinations will leave an indelible impression on your memories of the Isle of Man.

To enhance your exploration of the Isle of Man's seaside towns and villages, be sure to inquire about any special events, festivals, or cultural celebrations taking place during your visit, as these can offer a wonderful opportunity to experience the island's vibrant community spirit. Many of the island's coastal towns and villages are easily accessible by public transportation, including the Isle of Man Steam Railway and the island's extensive network of buses, making it easy to explore without a car.

Keep an eye out for local discounts and loyalty programs that can help you save on admission fees, dining, and shopping, particularly for Manx residents and frequent visitors.

Embrace the island's inherent sense of tranquility and slow down your pace of exploration, allowing yourself to fully immerse in the charm and character of each unique destination. Consider packing a picnic lunch or snacks to enjoy at one of the many scenic coastal viewpoints or harbor-side benches, allowing you to savor the island's natural beauty at your own leisure.

Outdoor Activities and Hiking Trails

The Isle of Man's captivating coastal landscapes and rugged interior offer an abundance of opportunities for outdoor enthusiasts and nature lovers to immerse themselves in the island's breathtaking natural splendor. Whether you're seeking a leisurely stroll along the shoreline or a challenging hike through the island's dramatic uplands, the Isle of Man promises to leave an indelible mark on your adventurous spirit.

The Millennium Way, a long-distance footpath that traverses the Manx uplands, is a popular hiking destination that allows visitors to explore the island's wild and untamed interior. The Millennium Way, which runs approximately 42 miles (68 kilometers) from Ramsey in the north to Port Erin in the south, takes hikers through a stunning succession of landscapes, from rugged moorlands and glacial valleys to the towering peaks of Snaefell and the Beinn y Phott range. Along the way, you'll be treated to breathtaking vistas that highlight the island's dramatic topography, including sweeping views of the Irish Sea and distant outlines of the Cumbrian fells across the water. For those looking for a more manageable day hike, consider one of the Millennium Way's many scenic sections, such as the Eairy to Snaefell leg or the Laxey to Lonan stretch, which each have their own distinct blend of natural wonders and cultural heritage.

Beyond the Millennium Way, you'll find a network of coastal walking trails that follow the island's captivating shoreline, providing unparalleled opportunities to immerse yourself in the Isle of Man's raw natural beauty. The Raad ny Foillan, or "Way of the Gull," is a 95-mile (153 km) trail that circles the entire island, showcasing the dramatic cliffs, secluded coves, and sweeping vistas that have long captivated visitors to this enchanting destination. For a more manageable coastal adventure, try the Isle of Man Coastal Path, which connects the island's picturesque seaside towns and villages, or go on a day hike through the Calf of Man nature reserve, where you can see a variety of seabirds, seals, and other marine wildlife.

Aside from the island's impressive network of hiking trails, the Isle of Man provides ample opportunities for outdoor enthusiasts to participate in a variety of other activities. For the more daring, consider taking a sea kayaking or stand-up paddleboarding excursion to explore the island's stunning coastline from a unique water-based perspective. Birdwatchers and wildlife enthusiasts will also enjoy the island's numerous nature reserves and designated Areas of Special Scientific Interest, which are home to a diverse range of avian species, as well as the enigmatic Manx cabbage, a rare endemic plant that clings tenaciously to the island's exposed cliffs and rocky outcrops.

Regardless of your preferred outdoor activity, the Isle of Man promises to captivate and inspire, with numerous opportunities to immerse yourself in the island's raw natural beauty and rich cultural history. So, lace up your hiking boots, grab your binoculars, and get ready for an unforgettable adventure that will leave you in awe of this enchanting island destination.

To enhance your outdoor adventures on the Isle of Man be sure to follow the following recommendations.

1. Be sure to pack appropriate clothing and footwear, as the island's weather can be unpredictable, with sudden changes in temperature and precipitation.
2. Consult local hiking guides or trail maps to plan your routes and familiarize yourself with the terrain and difficulty levels of the various trails.
3. Bring along a sturdy backpack, plenty of water and snacks, and any necessary safety gear, such as a first aid kit and a compass or GPS device.
4. Consider joining a guided hiking or outdoor tour, which can provide valuable insights into the island's history, ecology, and cultural traditions.
5. Respect the island's delicate natural environments and wildlife by adhering to established trails, staying on designated paths, and following all posted regulations and guidelines.

6. Embrace the island's inherent sense of tranquility and slow down your pace of exploration, allowing yourself to fully immerse in the beauty of your surroundings.

CHAPTER 4.

THE ISLE OF MAN'S UNIQUE HERITAGE

The Ancient Celtic and Norse Influences

The Isle of Man stands as a captivating tapestry of cultural influences, woven together over the centuries by the island's strategic location at the heart of the Irish Sea. At the core of this rich heritage are the enduring legacies of the island's ancient Celtic and Norse inhabitants, whose indelible mark can be traced through the island's archaeological sites, traditional customs, and enduring folklore.

The Celtic influence on the Isle of Man goes back thousands of years, to the arrival of the island's first known inhabitants, the Gaelic-speaking Celts. These brave settlers left an indelible mark on the Manx landscape, establishing fortified settlements, erecting impressive stone monuments, and cultivating a vibrant oral tradition that continues to captivate visitors today. One of the most impressive examples of the island's Celtic heritage is the Laxey Wheel, a 72-foot (22-meter) water wheel that was once used to pump water from nearby mines. This engineering marvel, affectionately known as "Lady Isabella," exemplifies the ingenuity and resourcefulness of the island's Celtic forefathers, who used the island's natural resources to support their thriving communities.

In addition to the Laxey Wheel, the Isle of Man has a plethora of other ancient Celtic sites that provide insight into the island's distant history. Tynwald Hill in the village of St. John's, for example, is thought to be the site of an ancient open-air parliament where the island's Celtic rulers would have met to discuss governance and justice. Nearby, the Balladoole archaeological site contains the ruins of an Iron Age hill fort, providing a tangible link to the island's Celtic warrior heritage. Further afield, the Meayll Peninsula is home to an impressive collection of Neolithic chambered tombs, serving as a poignant reminder of the island's first inhabitants and their reverence for nature.

The Norse influence on the Isle of Man is equally profound, dating back to the ninth century, when the island served as a strategic outpost for Viking settlers and raiders. The Manx language, a distinct Gaelic-Norse hybrid, exemplifies this cultural blending, with a vocabulary rich in Norse-derived words and a grammatical structure that reflects the island's position as a crossroads between the Celtic and Scandinavian worlds. Furthermore, the island's iconic Tynwald ceremony, a centuries-old tradition in which the island's laws are proclaimed in both Manx and English, is thought to have originated with Norse administrative practices prevalent during the Viking era.

The architectural heritage of the island reflects the influence of its Norse inhabitants, with the imposing Peel Castle standing out as a prime example. This impressive medieval fortress, perched atop a rocky headland on the island's western coast, was once the seat of the island's Norse rulers, and its architectural features, such as its striking curtain walls and strategic positioning, reflect the Viking settlers' military prowess and engineering expertise.

Beyond the tangible archaeological and architectural sites, the Isle of Man's rich tapestry of folklore and legends reflects the ancient Celtic and Norse influences. From the enigmatic Moddey Dhoo, a ghostly black hound said to haunt the corridors of Peel Castle, to the mischievous Phynnodderee, a hairy, elf-like creature that appears prominently in Manx mythology, the island's stories and legends provide a fascinating glimpse into the enduring cultural traditions that have shaped the Manx identity over the centuries.

As you explore the Isle of Man, you will hear echoes of its Celtic and Norse past, from the rugged landscapes left by ancient settlements to the enduring cultural practices that continue to shape the island's distinct character. Whether you're admiring the engineering feats of the island's Celtic forefathers or immersing yourself in the rich tapestry of Manx folklore and legends, the ancient influences that have shaped this captivating island destination will leave an indelible impression.

Castles, Forts, and Historic Manx Ruins

As you delve deeper into the Isle of Man's rich cultural tapestry, you'll be captivated by the island's impressive array of castles, forts, and historic ruins, each offering a unique window into the Manx past and the enduring legacies of its various ruling dynasties. These architectural marvels not only showcase the island's strategic importance throughout the centuries but also serve as powerful reminders of the Manx people's resilience and ingenuity in the face of ever-changing political and social landscapes.

Peel Castle, Isle of Man

One of the most recognizable and well-preserved of these historic sites is Peel Castle, a medieval fortress perched atop a rocky headland on the island's western coast. The castle, built by the Vikings in the 11th century, has striking curtain walls, defensive towers, and strategic positioning that reflect the island's Norse rulers' military prowess. Over the centuries, the castle has played an important role in the history of the Isle of Man, serving as a seat of power, a refuge, and a focal point for the island's maritime activities. Visitors can now explore the castle's atmospheric interiors, which include the haunting remains of a 14th-century cathedral and the legendary "Moddey Dhoo" - a ghostly black hound said to haunt the castle's corridors.

Castletown Castle, located further south, is one of the most impressive historic sites on the Isle of Man. This formidable fortress, which dates back to the 14th century, was once the island's government seat, housing the Lord Lieutenants and serving as a hub for the island's administrative and judicial functions. Today, visitors can wander through the castle's grand halls, explore its subterranean passages, and admire the architectural details that reflect the island's diverse cultural influences, ranging from sturdy medieval stonework to elegant Georgian-era additions. Be sure to stop by the nearby House of Manannan, an interactive museum that delves into the island's Celtic, Viking, and maritime legacies, providing valuable context and insights to help you explore this fascinating historic site.

Castletown Castle, le of Man

Further afield, you'll find a plethora of other historic ruins and fortifications dotting the Manx landscape, each with its own unique story to tell. The Langness Peninsula, located in the northeast of the island, contains remnants of a 19th-century coastal defense system, including artillery batteries, observation towers, and a striking lighthouse with panoramic views of the surrounding coastline. Meanwhile, in the island's central uplands, the ruins of Cronk yn Irree Laa serve as a reminder of the island's ancient Celtic heritage, with the crumbling walls and earthworks of this Iron Age hill fort providing a poignant connection to the island's distant past.

For a more immersive experience with the Isle of Man's architectural heritage, consider taking a guided tour or visiting one of the island's many historic house museums, such as the Milntown Estate in Ramsey or the Cregneash Folk Museum in Port St. Mary. These captivating destinations not only provide a deeper dive into the island's history, but also a one-of-a-kind opportunity to travel back in time and gain a better understanding of the Manx people's enduring traditions and way of life.

As you explore the Isle of Man's impressive collection of castles, forts, and historic ruins, remember to use caution and follow all safety guidelines, especially when visiting sites with uneven terrain or fragile structures. Consider bringing a sturdy pair of walking shoes, a hat, and sunscreen, as many of these historic sites are located in exposed outdoor settings that are prone to the island's notoriously unpredictable weather.

Whether you're admiring Peel Castle's strategic placement, delving into the mysteries of Castletown Castle, or exploring the crumbling remnants of the island's ancient Celtic settlements, the Isle of Man's captivating architectural heritage promises to transport you to a bygone era and leave an indelible mark on your understanding of this enchanting island destination.

Traditional Manx Crafts and Artisanry

The Isle of Man's rich cultural heritage is not only reflected in its impressive array of historic sites and ancient influences, but also in the vibrant tapestry of traditional crafts and artisanal practices that have been meticulously passed down through the generations. As you explore the island, you'll be captivated by the skilled artisans and enterprising creatives who are dedicated to preserving the Manx's unique artistic legacy, seamlessly blending age-old techniques with contemporary design sensibilities.

The intricate art of Lace Making, which dates back to the island's textile industry in the 18th century, is one of the most iconic and enduring Manx crafts. Manx Lace, known for its delicate patterns and intricate stitchwork, was once popular throughout Europe, adorning nobility's garments and the interiors of grand estates. Today, a dedicated community of Manx Lace makers continues to preserve this timeless craft, with several island-based workshops and studios where visitors can witness the creation of these exquisite textiles firsthand. Visit the Laxey Lace Gallery in the picturesque village of Laxey, where you can admire the stunning work of local lace makers and even take an introductory class to learn how to make this delicate art form.

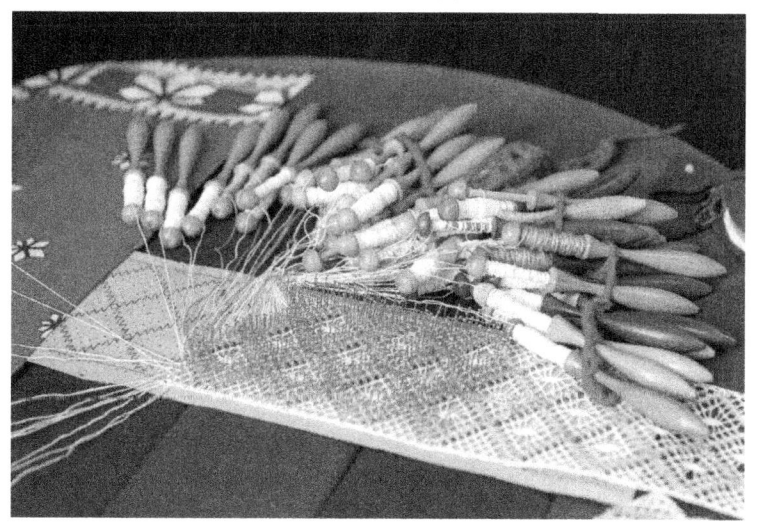

Along with the time-honored craft of lace making, the Isle of Man is also known for its exceptional knitwear, which is inspired by the island's rugged coastal landscapes and the resourcefulness of its seafaring inhabitants. Manx knitters have long been skilled at creating warm, weather-resistant garments from the fine wool of the island's iconic Manx Loghtan sheep, a hardy breed that has inhabited the Manx uplands for centuries. Today, the island is home to a thriving community of independent knitwear designers and producers, each with their own distinct take on traditional Manx patterns and techniques. Visit the Manx Woollens showroom in Peel to browse a carefully curated selection of locally made sweaters, scarves, and accessories, or consider taking a hands-on knitting workshop to learn the secrets of this time-honored Manx craft.

Beyond the textile arts, the Isle of Man has a thriving community of potters, glassblowers, and other artisanal producers who all contribute to the island's rich creative legacy. The Niarbyl Pottery Studio in the picturesque seaside town of Port Erin showcases the exceptional work of local ceramicists who are inspired by the island's coastal landscapes to create stunning, functional pieces that celebrate the Manx aesthetic. Meanwhile, in Douglas, the Manx Glass Studio allows visitors to witness the mesmerizing art of glassblowing, where skilled artisans transform molten glass into intricate, one-of-a-kind sculptures and decorative pieces.

For a more in-depth look at the Isle of Man's artistic heritage, visit the Manx Museum in Douglas, which houses a fascinating collection of traditional crafts and artworks from the island's long and illustrious history. Here, you'll find exquisite examples of Manx Lace, Knitwear, and Metalwork, as well as a wealth of information about the island's talented community of contemporary creatives who are committed to preserving and reinventing these timeless artistic traditions.

As you explore the Isle of Man's vibrant creative landscape, take the time to interact with the island's skilled artisans, learn about their techniques and inspirations, and perhaps even participate in a hands-on workshop or demonstration. By doing so, you will not only deepen your appreciation for the Manx's enduring artistic legacy, but will also help to ensure that these time-honored crafts and practices continue to thrive for future generations.

Manx National Heritage Sites

One of the greatest ways to become fully immersed in the Isle of Man's enduring legacy as you delve deeper into its rich cultural tapestry is to visit its network of Manx National Heritage sites. Visitors can travel back in time at these painstakingly restored and skillfully curated locations, which reveal the Manx's colorful past through captivating live interpretations, interactive exhibits, and engaging exhibits.

The Manx Museum in Douglas is at the heart of this impressive network of heritage sites, serving as the island's primary repository of cultural, historical, and archaeological treasures. The Manx Museum, housed in a striking neoclassical building, provides a comprehensive overview of the Isle of Man's captivating story, with exhibitions focusing on the island's Celtic and Norse influences, strategic importance over the centuries, and the rich tapestry of Manx customs and traditions. Allow plenty of time to explore the museum's diverse collection, which includes everything from ancient Celtic cross-slabs and Viking hoards to stunning examples of Manx lace and knitwear. Don't miss out on one of the museum's engaging talks or guided tours, where you'll learn valuable information from the island's top historians and cultural experts.

Beyond the Manx Museum, the island's network of National Heritage sites includes a plethora of other captivating destinations that highlight the Manx's enduring legacy. In the picturesque village of Cregneash, for example, the Cregneash Folk Museum provides visitors with a unique glimpse into the island's traditional way of life, complete with a collection of lovingly restored historic buildings and interactive demonstrations that bring the island's rural heritage to life. Wander through the museum's thatched cottages, watch the traditional Manx Lace making process, and perhaps even sample a delectable Manx delicacy, all while immersed in the enchanting atmosphere of this living history museum.

Other Manx National Heritage sites that celebrate the island's diverse cultural legacies include the imposing grandeur of Peel Castle and the medieval splendor of Rushen Abbey, as well as the interactive marvel of the House of Manannan in Castletown. At each of these meticulously preserved locations, you'll be able to engage with the island's past in engaging and thought-provoking ways, whether it's exploring the haunting corridors of a medieval fortress, discovering the secrets of an ancient monastic community, or delving into the island's Celtic and Norse roots through cutting-edge multimedia exhibits.

When planning your visit to the Isle of Man's National Heritage sites, make sure to check the Manx National Heritage website or pick up a comprehensive heritage guide to ensure you don't miss any of the island's must-see cultural attractions. Consider purchasing a Manx National Heritage Pass, which provides discounted admission to a number of the island's top heritage attractions and can help you make the most of your exploration of the Manx's fascinating history.

As you explore the Isle of Man's National Heritage sites, remember to approach them with curiosity and respect. Follow all posted guidelines and regulations, and keep in mind the island's historic structures and archaeological resources are fragile. You will not only gain a greater appreciation for the Manx's enduring cultural legacy, but you will also help to preserve these invaluable treasures for future generations to discover and cherish.

CHAPTER 5.

IMMERSING IN THE ISLAND'S NATURAL WONDERS

The Unspoiled Glens and Valleys

As you venture beyond the island's historic towns and cultural landmarks, the Isle of Man's natural wonders truly begin to take center stage, offering visitors a chance to immerse themselves in a breathtaking tapestry of unspoiled glens, dramatic valleys, and enchanting waterways. These captivating natural landscapes, sculpted by centuries of glacial activity and shaped by the island's ever-changing climatic conditions, are a testament to the Isle of Man's enduring geological and ecological legacy.

One of the most impressive and awe-inspiring of these natural wonders is the Laxey Glen, a verdant, U-shaped valley that cuts a dramatic path through the island's central uplands. The Laxey Glen, carved out by glaciers during the last ice age, is a true nature lover's paradise, with meandering streams, ancient woodland, and flourishing wildflower meadows providing a haven for a diverse array of plant and animal life. While exploring this captivating glen, keep an eye out for the elusive red-billed chough, a charismatic member of the crow family that has long been associated with the Manx landscape, as well as the island's iconic Manx Loghtan sheep, whose sturdy, surefooted presence has helped to shape the character of the island's upland pastures for centuries.

Going a little further north, you'll come across the Sulby Glen, a lush, river-carved valley that cuts a picturesque path through the island's rugged interior. The Sulby Glen, known for its dramatic waterfalls, tranquil pools, and towering, moss-covered rock formations, is a true paradise for outdoor enthusiasts and nature lovers alike. As you explore this enchanting destination, make sure to stop by Glen Dhoo, a captivating wooded ravine with the remnants of an ancient lead mine, a poignant reminder of the island's industrial past and its inhabitants' resourcefulness in harnessing the bounty of nature.

Further south, the Injebreck Valley entices with its distinct combination of natural wonders and cultural heritage. This picturesque glen, carved out by glaciers and shaped by the island's ancient Celtic inhabitants, contains the ruins of Odin's Hill, an Iron Age hill fort that serves as a tangible link to the island's distant past. As you walk through the valley's rolling meadows and shimmering streams, keep an eye out for the vibrant array of wildflowers and birdlife that thrive in this protected natural sanctuary, from the delicate blooms of the endemic Manx cabbage to the graceful aerial displays of the Manx shearwater, a seabird that nests in the island's coastal cliffs.

Aside from these captivating glens, the Isle of Man is home to a plethora of other natural wonders, including the dramatic Calf of Man, a small island that serves as a designated nature reserve, and the serene Ballaugh Curragh, a tranquil wetland that provides critical habitat for a diverse array of plant and animal species. Regardless of which of the island's natural landscapes you choose to explore, you'll have a truly immersive experience that honors the Isle of Man's long geological and ecological history.

When planning a visit to the Isle of Man's glens and valleys, bring sturdy hiking boots, weatherproof clothing, and a strong sense of adventure. Many of these destinations have rugged, uneven terrain and are subject to the island's notoriously unpredictable weather, so use caution and respect the delicate balance of these fragile natural environments. Consider taking a guided tour or purchasing a comprehensive hiking map to help you navigate these captivating landscapes, and remember to leave no trace as you explore to ensure that these unspoiled natural wonders are preserved and protected for future generations.

Immersing yourself in the Isle of Man's glens and valleys will not only deepen your appreciation for the island's raw natural beauty, but also provide you with a new understanding of the enduring forces that have shaped this captivating destination over millennia. So, lace up your boots, pack your supplies, and get ready to embark on an unforgettable journey through the Isle of Man's unspoiled natural beauty.

Birdwatching and Wildlife Spotting

For avid nature enthusiasts and passionate wildlife observers, the Isle of Man offers a truly unparalleled experience, boasting a diverse array of avian species and a wealth of captivating terrestrial and marine life that have long captivated visitors to this enchanting island destination. Whether you're an experienced birder seeking to add rare and elusive species to your life list or a budding naturalist eager to immerse yourself in the island's vibrant ecological tapestry, the Isle of Man promises to leave an indelible mark on your appreciation for the natural world.

The Calf of Man, a small, rugged island that serves as a designated nature reserve and home to a diverse range of seabirds and marine mammals, is central to the island's birdwatching and wildlife viewing opportunities. The Calf of Man, accessible via a short boat ride from the island's southern coast, is home to one of the world's largest colonies of Manx shearwaters, with tens of thousands of these graceful, black-and-white seabirds flocking to the island's steep cliffs each breeding season to raise their young. As you arrive on this enchanting island, keep an eye out for the sleek, agile flight of the Manx shearwater, as well as the raucous calls and acrobatic displays of other seabird species like the distinctive black-legged kittiwake, the elegant common tern, and the charismatic European shag.

Calf of Man

Beyond the avian wonders of the Calf of Man, the island's rugged coastline and sheltered bays provide critical habitat for a diverse range of marine mammals, including the playful common seal and the enigmatic Atlantic grey seal. With a little patience and a keen eye, you might even be able to spot the elusive harbor porpoise, a small cetacean that frequents the island's coastal waters, or catch a glimpse of the majestic basking shark, the world's second-largest fish, as it glides effortlessly through the surrounding seas.

When you venture inland, you'll discover that the Isle of Man's natural treasures extend far beyond its coastal landscapes, with the island's carefully protected national glens and upland habitats providing a haven for a diverse range of terrestrial wildlife. In the verdant Sulby Glen, for example, you may see the iconic red-billed chough, a member of the crow family that has long been associated with the Manx landscape, as well as the island's diminutive but resilient Manx Loghtan sheep grazing contentedly among the lush vegetation. Meanwhile, in the tranquil Ballaugh Curragh, a designated wetland reserve, you'll have the opportunity to see a variety of waterfowl and wading birds, including the graceful little egret and the elusive water rail.

For those looking to improve their wildlife viewing experiences, consider joining one of the island's expert-led birdwatching or nature tours, which provide insider knowledge and access to some of the Isle of Man's most secluded and wildlife-rich areas. Alternatively, you can visit the Manx Museum in Douglas, which has a wealth of information and interactive exhibits about the island's fascinating natural history and the diverse array of species that live here.

When embarking on wildlife viewing adventures, make sure to bring a pair of binoculars, a camera with a long lens, and a sturdy pair of walking shoes or boots. Furthermore, be aware of the delicate balance of the island's natural environments and follow all posted regulations and guidelines to ensure the ongoing protection and preservation of these invaluable ecological treasures. With patience, curiosity, and reverence, you'll be rewarded with an immersive and unforgettable encounter with the natural wonders of the Isle of Man - a truly remarkable experience that will leave an indelible mark on your heart and mind.

Scenic Coastal Paths and Nature Reserves

One of the most fascinating and satisfying parts of discovering the wonders of the Isle of Man will definitely be getting to walk along the well-kept network of picturesque coastal paths and spend time in the island's designated nature reserves. Visitors can witness the raw, untamed beauty of the Isle of Man and develop a deeper understanding of the delicate balance of its fragile ecosystems through these captivating natural landscapes, shaped over millennia by the relentless forces of wind, waves, and glacial activity.

One of the crown jewels of the Isle of Man's coastal walking trails is the renowned Raad ny Foillan, or "The Way of the Gull," a 95-mile (153-kilometer) long footpath that hugs the island's rugged perimeter, offering sweeping vistas of the shimmering Irish Sea and the gentle undulations of the Manx landscape. As you embark on this captivating journey, you'll be treated to a remarkable diversity of coastal habitats, from the towering sea cliffs of the island's northern shores, where colonies of seabirds such as the graceful kittiwake and the iconic Manx shearwater soar on the wind, to the tranquil, sandy beaches of the south, where you may catch a glimpse of the playful common seal or the enigmatic harbor porpoise frolicking in the tidal pools.

Go a little further south and you'll find the charming Calf of Man, a tiny, isolated island that's home to numerous rare and endangered species and is recognized as a nature reserve. The Calf of Man, which is easily reached by boat from the southwest coast of the island, is a real treasure for lovers of the natural world. Its remarkable variety of plants and animals has long drawn tourists to this alluring location. Keep an eye out for the island's impressive seabird colonies as you explore the rugged landscapes of the Calf. These include some of the world's largest Manx shearwater breeding grounds, as well as the elusive peregrine falcon and the charismatic chough, who have made this protected refuge their home.

The Isle of Man's coastline is dotted with numerous nature reserves and protected habitats beyond the Calf of Man, each with its own special combination of breathtaking scenery and natural wonders. With its expansive sand dunes, shimmering beaches, and tranquil lagoons, the Ayres National Nature Reserve in the north is a veritable paradise for lovers of birds and other wildlife. It serves as a vital haven for a wide variety of resident and migratory bird species. A wealth of waterfowl and wading birds, from the majestic little egret to the elusive water rail, depend on the tranquil oasis of marshes, streams, and reedbeds that is the Ballaugh Curragh Wetland Reserve on the eastern shores of the island.

Take along waterproof clothing, sturdy hiking boots, and a strong sense of adventure when you explore the Isle of Man's beautiful coastal paths and nature reserves. Being mindful of the delicate balance of these fragile natural environments is important, as many of these destinations have rugged, uneven terrain and are susceptible to the notoriously unpredictable weather on the island. To help you navigate these fascinating landscapes, think about signing up for a guided tour or getting a detailed hiking map. Remember to leave no trace when you explore to help preserve these pristine, unspoiled natural wonders for future generations.

You will develop a deeper appreciation for the island's unadulterated natural beauty as well as a fresh perspective on the enduring forces that have shaped this alluring destination over millennia by immersing yourself in the nature reserves and coastal paths of the Isle of Man. So grab your gear, lace up your boots, and get ready for an incredible journey through the stunning shoreline and natural wonders of the Isle of Man.

Outdoor Recreational Activities

Deeper exploration of the Isle of Man's natural treasures reveals that this alluring island destination has much more to offer than just stunning scenery and a wealth of wildlife. The Isle of Man offers an exciting range of outdoor recreational activities that appeal to adventurers and outdoor enthusiasts of all stripes, beyond its breathtaking coastal paths, tranquil glens, and protected nature reserves. These activities are guaranteed to provide an exhilarating experience that will leave a lasting impression on even the most seasoned thrill-seeker.

For those looking to test their physical limits and embrace the island's more rugged terrain, the Isle of Man's network of hiking trails and fell-running routes will provide an exhilarating challenge. Lace up your boots and take on the Raad ny Foillan, the island's renowned "Way of the Gull" coastal path, which winds its way along the island's dramatic shoreline, providing breathtaking views and the opportunity to see a variety of seabirds and marine life. Alternatively, put your skills to the test on the Millennium Way, a strenuous 42-mile (68-kilometer) trail that winds through the island's central uplands, providing hikers with a mesmerizing tapestry of rolling moorlands, ancient stone walls, and the occasional herd of Manx Loghtan sheep.

Sea Kayaking

If you prefer adrenaline-fueled activities, the Isle of Man promises to deliver with its exciting range of water sports and outdoor adventures. Try your hand at sea kayaking, navigating the shimmering bays and hidden coves along the Manx coastline. For the ultimate adrenaline rush, board a powerboat or take to the skies on a paragliding or hang-gliding adventure, soaring high above the island's dramatic landscapes and admiring the breathtaking panoramic vistas that stretch out to the distant horizon.

If you prefer a more serene and contemplative outdoor experience, the Isle of Man has you covered as well. Take a leisurely birdwatching expedition through the island's tranquil glens and nature reserves, looking for the elusive Manx shearwater, the majestic peregrine falcon, and the island's iconic red-billed chough. Alternatively, try your hand at fly-fishing, casting your line into the island's tranquil rivers and streams in search of the prized brown trout that have long captivated the island's anglers.

Whatever your preferred outdoor activity, the Isle of Man guarantees an unforgettable experience that celebrates the island's raw natural beauty as well as the limitless opportunities for adventure and exploration it provides. Consider consulting with one of the island's experienced outdoor activity providers to help plan your itinerary, or purchase a comprehensive outdoor recreation guide to ensure you don't miss out on any of the Manx's must-see destinations and adrenaline-fueled activities.

As you enjoy the Isle of Man's outdoor recreational opportunities, remember to be cautious, respect the island's fragile ecosystems, and follow all safety guidelines and regulations. Many of these activities, from fell-running to sea kayaking, involve inherent risks, so it is critical to arrive prepared with the necessary equipment, skills, and knowledge to ensure a safe and enjoyable experience. By doing so, you will not only create lasting memories of your Manx adventure, but will also help to preserve the island's natural wonders for future generations.

So, whether you want to test your physical limits, immerse yourself in the island's captivating wildlife, or simply enjoy the serene beauty of the Manx landscape, the Isle of Man's outdoor recreational opportunities promise to provide an unforgettable experience that will leave an indelible mark on your heart and mind.

CHAPTER 6.

EXPLORING THE ISLE OF MAN'S RURAL HEARTLAND

Quaint Manx Villages and Hamlets

As you venture beyond the island's bustling towns and cultural hubs, the true essence of the Isle of Man begins to reveal itself in the form of its captivating rural villages and picturesque hamlets. These charming, time-honored settlements, nestled amidst the island's rolling hills, lush glens, and rugged coastlines, offer visitors a chance to immerse themselves in the Manx's enduring pastoral heritage and witness the enduring traditions that have shaped the character of this unique island destination.

Cregneash, a living history museum that offers a fascinating glimpse into the island's traditional way of life, is a must-see on your journey. Strolling through the village's lovingly restored thatched cottages and winding lanes will transport you back in time, where you'll meet skilled artisans working on time-honored crafts like Manx lace and traditional weaving. Make sure to visit the Cregneash Folk Museum, which has a wealth of interactive exhibits and demonstrations that bring the island's rural heritage to life, from the rhythmic clopping of heavy Shire horses to the sights and sounds of a fully operational 19th-century Manx farm.

Cregneash, cottages in Isle of Man

Further north, the picturesque village of Laxey entices with its distinct blend of natural beauty and cultural charm. This captivating destination, located in the heart of the Laxey Valley, is best known for its iconic Laxey Wheel, a magnificent 72-foot-tall (22-meter) water wheel that once powered the island's thriving mining industry. As you explore the village, make sure to stop by the Laxey Woollen Mills to see how the island's famous Manx knitwear is made, and the Laxey Lace Gallery to see the intricate handiwork of the island's skilled lace makers.

As you travel deeper into the island's rural heartland, you will come across a tapestry of other quaint Manx villages and hamlets, each with its own unique character and cultural treasures. The Manx Museum, a fascinating repository of the island's rich history and cultural legacy, is located in the charming seaside town of Peel, as is the iconic Peel Castle, a striking medieval fortress that stands as a testament to the island's strategic importance over the centuries. Further south, the picturesque village of Port Erin is home to a plethora of natural wonders, including the tranquil Niarbyl Bay and the dramatic sea cliffs that have long captivated visitors to this enchanting corner of the island.

When planning your trip to the Isle of Man's quaint rural villages and hamlets, consult the island's comprehensive visitor information resources to ensure you don't miss any of the must-see attractions. Consider purchasing a detailed map or downloading a digital guide to help you navigate the island's winding country roads and narrow village lanes, and make sure to leave plenty of time to fully immerse yourself in each destination's distinct character and captivating charms.

As you travel through the Manx countryside, remember to approach each village and hamlet with respect and curiosity. Engage with the friendly locals, visit the independent shops and eateries that showcase the island's culinary and craft traditions, and keep in mind the island's historic structures and natural environments are fragile. By doing so, you will not only increase your appreciation for the Isle of Man's enduring rural heritage, but you will also help to ensure that these captivating destinations thrive and evolve for future generations.

So put on your walking shoes, pack a picnic basket, and prepare to embark on a captivating adventure through the Isle of Man's quaint rural heartland, where time-honored traditions, natural beauty, and the enduring spirit of the Manx people come together to create an unforgettable experience that will leave an indelible mark on your soul.

Agricultural Experiences and Farm Visits

One of the most fascinating and immersive ways to experience the island's long-standing pastoral traditions is to pay a visit to one of the many family-run farms or agricultural businesses in the rural heartland of the Isle of Man. Generations of Manx farmers have meticulously cultivated and tended these working landscapes, providing visitors with a rare chance to observe the island's age-old agricultural methods, develop a greater understanding of the island's rich culinary legacy, and create lifelong bonds with the land and its people.

One of the most iconic and beloved agricultural experiences on the Isle of Man is a visit to a traditional Manx sheep farm, where you can meet the island's famous Manx Loghtan breed. These hardy, horned sheep, with their distinctive dark fleece and sturdy, agile build, have long been an important part of the Manx landscape, with their grazing habits influencing the character of the island's rolling upland pastures. At a Manx sheep farm, you can observe the shepherds' daily routines, which include carefully tending to their flocks, shearing the sheep, and processing the precious wool that has been used to craft the island's renowned Manx knitwear for generations.

Farm fields in the Isle of Man

Beyond sheep farming, the Isle of Man has a thriving community of dairy and livestock producers, each with their own unique perspective on the island's agricultural heritage. Visit a family-owned dairy farm and see the time-honored process of milk production, from gentle milking of the cows to the creation of the island's famous Manx cheeses and dairy products. Alternatively, immerse yourself in the world of rare-breed pig farming, where you'll be able to interact with the island's iconic Manx Loaghtan pigs, whose distinct appearance and flavorful meat have made them a beloved part of Manx cuisine.

For those with a green thumb, the Isle of Man's network of family-owned produce farms and market gardens provides a fascinating glimpse into the island's thriving horticultural heritage. Visit a sprawling potato farm and witness the time-honored process of hand-harvesting the island's renowned "Queenies" - a prized variety grown on the Manx for centuries. Explore the verdant rows of a family-run market garden, where you can pick your own seasonal produce while learning about the island's sustainable farming practices.

Regardless of which agricultural experience you choose, one thing is certain: you will have a truly immersive and unforgettable experience that honors the enduring spirit of the Manx farming community and the island's deep connection to the land. Consider contacting the Isle of Man's network of farm stay accommodations to plan a longer visit where you can fully immerse yourself in the rhythm of farm life and gain a firsthand understanding of the challenges and joys of being a Manx farmer.

As you explore the island's agricultural enterprises, keep in mind how fragile these working landscapes are and how important it is to respect the privacy and livelihoods of the families who live there. Follow all posted guidelines and regulations, and come prepared to participate in any hands-on activities or chores that may be part of the visitor experience. By doing so, you will not only increase your appreciation for the Isle of Man's rich agricultural heritage, but you will also help to support the island's thriving rural economy and ensure the preservation of these captivating cultural touchstones.

So, put on your wellies, roll up your sleeves, and get ready to embark on an unforgettable agricultural adventure that will leave an indelible mark on your heart and mind as you discover the raw, captivating essence of the Isle of Man's rural heart.

Traditional Manx Pubs and Eateries

Immersion in the island's vibrant pub culture and rich culinary heritage will undoubtedly be one of the most captivating and rewarding aspects of your journey as you venture deeper into the rural heart of the Isle of Man. The Isle of Man's traditional pubs and locally sourced eateries give guests an opportunity to experience the flavors that have sustained the Manx people for generations. These establishments range from warm, traditional ones serving up classic Manx fare to cutting-edge eateries showcasing the island's contemporary culinary talents.

Traditional Manx pubs are at the forefront of the island's renowned culinary scene, having long served as the beating heart of the island's rural communities. Stepping into the welcoming embrace of a charming country inn, such as the Creg-ny-Baa in Laxey or the Trafalgar in Port Erin, you'll be greeted by the warm, convivial atmosphere that has made these establishments a popular gathering place for both locals and visitors. Sip on a pint of locally brewed Manx beer, such as the award-winning Bushy's ale, while enjoying the pub's time-honored ambiance, which includes roaring fires, cozy nooks, and walls adorned with fascinating historical memorabilia.

However, the true culinary jewel in the Isle of Man's crown is its abundance of locally sourced, farm-to-table restaurants that celebrate the island's rich agricultural heritage with each bite. Visit the Laxey Woollen Mills Café for a hearty Manx breakfast of fresh-baked Manx kippers, fluffy Manx-farmed eggs, and the island's famous Queenie potatoes, or step into the rustic charm of

Peel's Creggans Restaurant, where the menu highlights the bounty of the island's surrounding seas and farms, from succulent Manx-reared lamb to the freshest locally caught seafood.

For a truly immersive dining experience that honors the island's deep-rooted culinary traditions, look into one of the Isle of Man's family-run farmhouse kitchens or heritage-focused cooking schools. At places like the Ballamoar Farmhouse in Foxdale and the Milntown Cookery School in Ramsey, you can learn time-honored techniques and recipes passed down through generations of Manx cooks, all while savoring the rich, intensely flavorful ingredients grown on the island's verdant landscapes.

When planning your culinary adventures on the Isle of Man, make sure to consult the island's extensive visitor resources to find the best traditional pubs and locally sourced restaurants. Many of these establishments provide unique tasting menus, interactive demonstrations, and opportunities to connect directly with the island's food producers, allowing you to gain a better understanding of the Manx's enduring culinary legacy.

Remember to approach these dining experiences with openness and curiosity, and interact with the passionate, knowledgeable staff who can tell you about the island's signature dishes and traditional preparation methods. You'll not only enjoy the exceptional flavors of the Manx, but you'll also develop a strong connection to the land, the people, and the enduring traditions that have shaped this captivating island destination for centuries.

So, come with an empty stomach and an open mind, and get ready to embark on a culinary journey that will tantalize your taste buds, nourish your soul, and leave an indelible mark on your Isle of Man memories.

Scenic Inland Drives and Hiking Trails

You will be rewarded with an amazing tapestry of picturesque inland drives and well-maintained hiking trails that offer unrivaled opportunities to immerse yourself in the island's pastoral charms as you venture beyond the captivating coastal regions of the Isle of Man and into the island's rural landscapes. The Isle of Man's network of inland routes and hiking paths promises to deliver an unforgettable experience that celebrates the raw, natural beauty of this enchanting island destination, whether you're looking for a leisurely sightseeing excursion or a more strenuous outdoor adventure.

The Eairy Cushlin Raad, or "Road of the Eternal Glens," is a winding, 26-mile (42-kilometer) route that meanders through the island's verdant central uplands, allowing visitors to witness the rugged grandeur of the Manx landscape in all its glory. As you travel this captivating route, you'll be treated to a breathtaking view of rolling moorlands, ancient stone walls, and the occasional herd of the island's iconic Manx Loghtan sheep, all set against the backdrop of the island's dramatic central peaks, including the iconic summit of Snaefell, the island's highest point.

For those looking for a more immersive outdoor experience, the Isle of Man's network of hiking trails promises to provide numerous opportunities to explore the island's pastoral landscapes on foot. The Millennium Way, a strenuous 42-mile (68-kilometer) trail that traverses the island's central uplands, offers hikers a captivating blend of natural wonders, from the serene glens and cascading waterfalls of the island's northern reaches to the rugged, wind-swept moorlands of the south. As you embark on this epic journey, prepare to be rewarded with breathtaking views, the opportunity to see a variety of native Manx wildlife, and a profound sense of connection to the island's long-standing pastoral heritage.

Beyond the Millennium Way, the Isle of Man offers a plethora of other hiking trails and scenic walking routes suitable for adventurers of all skill levels. The Dhoon Glen Loop in the island's north offers a captivating blend of natural beauty and cultural significance, as you navigate a gently winding path past the breathtaking Dhoon Waterfall and the ruins of the historic Dhoon Mill. Meanwhile, in the island's south, the Raad ny Foillan coastal path intersects with a network of inland trails that allow hikers to explore the island's pastoral heartland, from the quaint villages of the Calf Peninsula to the sweeping panoramas of the Cregneash Uplands.

Regardless of which inland driving route or hiking trail you choose, one thing is certain: you will have an unforgettable experience that celebrates the Isle of Man's raw, natural beauty and the enduring connection between its people and the land that has supported them for generations. Consider using the island's extensive visitor resources to plan your itinerary, and make sure to bring the necessary gear, provisions, and safety equipment to ensure a safe and enjoyable trip.

As you explore the Isle of Man's inland landscapes, remember to be cautious, respect the island's fragile ecosystems, and leave no trace to ensure that these captivating natural wonders are preserved and protected for future generations. With a spirit of curiosity, adventure, and reverence, you'll be rewarded with a deep and lasting connection to the heart and soul of this enchanting island destination.

CHAPTER 7.

TRANSPORT AND GETTING AROUND

The Isle of Man's Road Network

As you prepare to embark on your adventure through the Isle of Man, one of the first and most crucial aspects of your journey will be mastering the art of navigating the island's unique and captivating road network. Unlike the broad, sweeping highways that characterize many modern travel destinations, the Isle of Man's roads are a reflection of the island's rugged, pastoral landscape, winding their way through a tapestry of rolling hills, narrow glens, and picturesque villages, offering visitors a truly immersive experience that celebrates the island's enduring charm and character.

The vast A- and B-road network that connects the island's main towns and tourist destinations spans more than 300 miles (480 kilometers) and forms the backbone of the Isle of Man's transportation system. These routes, many of which are centuries old, are well known for their breathtaking scenery and for taking visitors on a journey through time as they wind through an area peppered with medieval castles, charming Manx villages, and old stone walls.

The island's renowned narrow and winding roads are among the most alluring features of driving on the Isle of Man; visitors used to the wider, straighter highways of the mainland may find them to be a particular challenge. Prepare yourself for a multitude of unexpected obstacles as you travel these fascinating routes, such as steep gradients and sharp hairpin turns, as well as the occasional flock of sheep or herd of Manx Loghtan cattle that may wander onto the road without warning. These distinctive features, which at first glance may seem intimidating, add to the island's timeless charm and character and give drivers an opportunity to slow down, enjoy the scenery, and fully immerse themselves in the Manx way of life.

You must be well-prepared and have a thorough awareness of the driving customs and traffic laws of the Isle of Man in order to guarantee a safe and enjoyable driving experience. Some visitors may be surprised to learn that the Isle of Man drives on the left side of the road, in contrast to many other destinations. It's also crucial to be alert and follow the posted signage because the island's speed limits, which vary from 15 mph (24 km/h) in some villages to 60 mph (96 km/h) on the open roads, are strictly enforced.

Renting a car that is appropriate for the driving conditions on the island is one of the best ways to handle the winding roads of the Isle of Man with assurance and comfort. Compact or mid-size vehicles are popular among tourists because they are easier to maneuver and park in the charming village centers of the island. Alternatively, the Isle of Man's system of unpaved roads and isolated rural landscapes may require the extra capability and ground clearance of a four-wheel-drive vehicle for those looking for a more daring driving experience.

Driving on the Isle of Man can be successful and enjoyable, no matter what kind of vehicle you choose, as long as you approach the journey with patience, caution, and a steadfast appreciation for the island's breathtaking scenery. Be patient, stop to enjoy the view, and be ready to yield to the odd passing tractor or straggling sheep. By doing this, you'll guarantee a worry-free and safe travel as well as make priceless memories of your thorough investigation of this genuinely remarkable and enchanted island location.

Public Transportation Options

While the Isle of Man's winding rural roads and captivating scenic drives undoubtedly offer a thrilling and immersive way to explore the island, the destination also boasts a well-developed public transportation network that provides visitors with a wealth of alternative mobility options, allowing them to sit back, relax, and soak in the island's mesmerizing landscapes without the hassle of navigating the roads themselves.

Buses are the backbone of the Isle of Man's public transport system, providing a thorough and incredibly effective means of getting around the island. With routes winding through the island's rural heartland and along the dramatic coastline, the Manx Bus service, run by the Department of Infrastructure on the island, connects the major towns and villages and gives passengers a front-row seat to the island's natural wonders. The Manx Bus network provides a dependable, reasonably priced, and environmentally responsible means of transportation, whether you're looking to explore the quaint seaside town of Peel, visit the enthralling glens of the island's central uplands, or just simply shuttle between your accommodations and the island's top attractions.

The Isle of Man is home to a cherished historic railway system that has been enthralling tourists for many years, making it an ideal choice for those looking for a more distinctive and nostalgic form of transportation. Operating continuously since 1893, the Manx Electric Railway is an iconic part of the island. Passengers can enjoy a delightful vintage tram experience as it transports them between the northern towns of Douglas and Ramsey, offering stunning views of the island's rolling countryside and dramatic coastline. Similarly, the 1873-founded Isle of Man Steam Railway offers a fascinating trip through the southern parts of the island; its meticulously restored Victorian-era coaches and locomotives are a real throwback to bygone eras.

In addition to the bus and rail systems on the island, there are numerous other public transportation options available in the Isle of Man, each with a distinct personality and appeal. Take the famous Snaefell Mountain Railway, which takes visitors to the summit of Snaefell, the island's highest point, where they can enjoy breath-taking 360-degree views of the Manx landscape, for a truly unique experience. Alternatively, embark on an exciting nautical voyage with the Isle of Man Steam Packet Company. This company offers a fleet of high-speed ferries that connect the island to both the United Kingdom and Ireland, making it possible for visitors to arrive in style and start their Manx adventure.

Regardless of the public transportation option you select, one thing is certain: while taking advantage of the convenience, comfort, and environmental friendliness that these modes of transportation offer, visitors to the Isle of Man will have an abundance of opportunities to explore the island's captivating landscapes and immerse themselves in its rich cultural heritage.

In order to familiarize yourself with the various public transportation options and to map out the best routes and schedules to suit your itinerary, make sure to consult the extensive visitor resources available on the island when you are planning your Manx adventure. You can easily and affordably navigate the island with the help of these services, many of which offer discounted tickets and multimodal passes. And don't forget to sit back, unwind, and enjoy the constantly shifting scenery as you travel through the Manx countryside. Let the island's timeless charm and natural beauty enthrall your senses and uplift your spirit.

Scenic Rail and Tram Services

Immersion in the island's beloved and historic rail and tram services is one of the most iconic and unforgettable ways to experience the captivating landscapes of the Isle of Man as you plan your adventure. Experience the raw, unadulterated beauty of the Manx countryside while indulging in a hint of nostalgic charm with these scenic transportation options, which range from the vintage charm of the Manx Electric Railway to the breathtaking ascent of the Snaefell Mountain Railway.

The Manx Electric Railway, a beloved institution that has been carrying passengers between the island's northern towns of Douglas and Ramsey since 1893, is arguably the most well-known of the Isle of Man's scenic rail experiences. Visitors are treated to an enthralling journey hugging the dramatic coastline, offering breathtaking views of the Irish Sea, the Calf of Man, and the island's rugged cliffs and coves, all from the comfort of the railway's lovingly restored, heritage-style trams. You will feel as though you have traveled back in time as you sway and clatter along the Manx Electric Railway's gently winding tracks. The rich, warm wood tones and elaborate brass fittings that have defined the railway's timeless aesthetic for well over a century are all around you.

The Isle of Man Steam Railway is an incredible experience that honors the island's pastoral heritage and is ideal for those looking for a more demanding and thrilling rail adventure. This historic narrow-gauge railway, which dates back to 1873, winds through a tapestry of rolling hills, ancient stone walls, and quaint Manx villages to link the island's southern town of Douglas with the picturesque coastal resort of Port Erin. You'll be treated to a captivating panorama of the island's lush landscapes as you travel aboard the railway's painstakingly restored Victorian-era locomotives and coaches, interspersed with the haunting whistle of the steam engine and the rhythmic clacking of the rails.

The Snaefell Mountain Railway is one of the island's most distinctive and alluring modes of transportation, in addition to the well-liked rail services. Operating continuously since 1895, this historic electric railway allows visitors to reach the summit of Snaefell, the island's highest point, at an astounding 2,036 feet (621 meters) above sea level. Passengers are treated to a captivating panorama that includes the island's rolling hills, dramatic coastlines, and, on a clear day, the distant shores of the United Kingdom, Ireland, Scotland, and even the Isle of Man's own Calf of Man, as the railway's gently sloping cars climb the mountain's winding tracks.

Make sure you familiarize yourself with the different routes, schedules, and ticketing options by consulting the comprehensive visitor resources of the Isle of Man when making travel plans on the scenic rail and tram services. Including these fascinating transportation options in your overall Manx adventure is made simple and affordable by the fact that many of these services offer discounted fares and multimodal passes. Plan your rail or tram ride to coincide with special occasions or seasonal highlights, like the magnificent autumnal foliage displays at the Snaefell Mountain Railway or the yearly "Illuminations" display of the Manx Electric Railway.

One thing is certain: you will be treated to an amazing journey that celebrates the island's rich heritage, captivating natural beauty, and enduring spirit of adventure, regardless of which scenic rail or tram experience you choose to take. So grab a picnic basket, lace up your walking shoes, and get ready to explore the genuine spirit of this fascinating island getaway while losing yourself in the ageless allure of the Isle of Man's most cherished transportation icons.

Ferries and Air Travel to the Island

One of the first and most important decisions you'll need to make as you get ready to travel to the Isle of Man is how to get to this alluring island destination. Thankfully, there is a wide variety of transportation available to visitors on the Isle of Man, including air and ferry travel, each with special benefits and experiences.

For those looking for a more traditional and nostalgic mode of transportation, the Isle of Man's ferry services, run by the renowned Isle of Man Steam Packet Company, provide a captivating nautical journey that has been a staple of the island's transportation network for generations. The company's fleet of high-speed passenger and vehicle ferries connects the Isle of Man to a number of destinations in the United Kingdom and Ireland, including Liverpool, Heysham, Dublin, and Belfast, offering visitors a comfortable and scenic journey to the island's shores.

One of the primary benefits of traveling to the Isle of Man by ferry is the opportunity to see the island's dramatic coastline from a unique perspective. As your ferry travels through the Irish Sea, you'll be treated to breathtaking views of the island's rugged cliffs, secluded coves, and picturesque harbors, laying the groundwork for an immersive and captivating start to your Manx journey. Furthermore, the ferry services provide a variety of on-board amenities, including cozy lounges and restaurants, duty-free shopping, and children's play areas, ensuring a comfortable and enjoyable journey for passengers of all ages and interests.

For those who prefer the speed and convenience of air travel, the Isle of Man has a well-connected international airport located near the island's capital, Douglas. The Isle of Man Airport (IATA code: IOM) operates regular scheduled flights to and from a number of destinations in the United Kingdom and Ireland, providing visitors with a convenient and efficient means of getting to the island. Whether you're flying in from London, Manchester, Dublin, or elsewhere, the airport's modern amenities and user-friendly layout ensure a stress-free and hassle-free arrival.

One of the primary advantages of flying to the Isle of Man is the speed and convenience of the trip. With flight times from many major UK and Irish airports of less than an hour, you'll be able to make the most of your time on the island rather than spending hours traveling. Furthermore, the island's airport offers a variety of on-site amenities, such as car rental services, public transportation connections, and even a heritage railway station, allowing you to seamlessly transition from the runway to your larger Manx journey.

Whether you arrive on the Isle of Man by ferry or by air, one thing is certain: you will be treated to a captivating and memorable journey that will set the tone for an unforgettable exploration of this enchanting island destination. Make sure to research and book your transportation well in advance, as ferry and air services can be in high demand during peak travel seasons. Consider the various package deals and multimodal options available, which can often result in significant cost savings and added convenience for your entire Manx adventure.

As you plan your trip to the Isle of Man, remember the spirit of exploration and adventure that has long defined this fascinating island. Whether you choose the timeless charm of a ferry crossing or the speed and efficiency of air travel, you can be confident that your arrival on Manx shores will mark the beginning of an unforgettable and immersive experience that celebrates the island's rich heritage, breathtaking natural beauty, and enduring spirit.

CHAPTER 8.

FESTIVALS, EVENTS, AND ENTERTAINMENT

Annual Festivals and Cultural Celebrations

As you plan your visit to the enchanting Isle of Man, be prepared to be captivated by the island's rich tapestry of annual festivals and cultural celebrations that showcase the Manx people's deep-rooted traditions, artistic talents, and enduring spirit of community. From the adrenaline-fueled Isle of Man TT Races to the vibrant celebrations of Manx heritage, these events offer visitors a unique opportunity to immerse themselves in the very heart and soul of this island paradise.

The annual Isle of Man TT (Tourist Trophy) Races, a world-famous motorcycle racing festival that has enthralled fans since 1907, is one of the island's most well-known and anticipated events. This exhilarating extravaganza, held every two weeks in June, draws legions of motorsports enthusiasts from all over the world to witness the sheer skill and bravery of the world's top motorcycle racers as they navigate the island's legendary 37.73-mile (60.72-kilometer) Mountain Course. For the best experience, we recommend purchasing your tickets and accommodations well in advance, as this event is extremely popular and can sell out fast.

Once on the island, immerse yourself in the electric atmosphere, explore the event's interactive exhibits and vendor stalls, and even consider taking a tour of the iconic Snaefell Mountain Course to get a sense of the full scale of this legendary racing circuit.

For a more serene and culturally enriching experience, plan your visit around the annual Manx National Festival, a vibrant two-week celebration of Manx music, dance, and language held in June. This popular event includes a variety of traditional performances, workshops, and competitions, allowing visitors to experience the island's enduring Gaelic traditions in all their glory. We recommend attending some of the festival's main events, such as the lively Manx music and dance competitions, where you can admire the intricate footwork of Manx dancers and the soulful harmonies of traditional Manx ballads. Consider participating in some of the festival's hands-on workshops, such as learning to play the traditional Manx harp or taking Gaelic language lessons.

As the year progresses, the Isle of Man's festival calendar continues to provide a plethora of exciting cultural events. The vibrant Peel

Carnival, held in July, celebrates the island's rich seafaring heritage through colorful parades, lively music, and traditional maritime activities. For a truly immersive experience, we recommend arriving early to secure a prime viewing spot along the parade route, followed by an exploration of the carnival's bustling vendor stalls and artisan craft demonstrations. Meanwhile, in August, the enchanting Laxey Woollen Mill Festival allows visitors to learn about the island's rich textile-making traditions through guided tours of the historic mill, live demonstrations of traditional weaving techniques, and the opportunity to purchase unique, locally-made Manx woolen goods.

As the seasons change and the days shorten, the island's annual Hop-tu-Naa festival in late October offers a captivating blend of ancient Celtic traditions and modern revelry. This New Year's celebration includes traditional songs, games, and the lighting of the iconic "oie Houney" bonfire, allowing visitors to witness the Manx people's strong connection to their island's heritage. To make the most of this event, arrive early to get a good spot near the bonfire, and then join in the lively festivities, which frequently include traditional Manx music, dance, and storytelling performances.

Regardless of which Manx festival you attend, you can expect an unforgettable and immersive celebration that highlights the island's rich cultural traditions, artistic talents, and enduring spirit of community. To plan your itinerary, consult the island's comprehensive event calendars and visitor resources, and remember to embrace the spirit of curiosity, openness, and reverence that will allow you to create lasting memories of your visit to this enchanting island.

Outdoor Concerts and Live Music Venues

Discover how the vibrant and diverse live music scene on the enchanted Isle of Man contributes to the island's rich cultural tapestry, which provides visitors with endless opportunities to experience the island's artistic talent and lively spirit. These are just a few examples of the many ways that the island's rich heritage and annual festivals are woven together.

One of the highlights of the Isle of Man's live music offerings is its outdoor concert series, which takes place at various picturesque locations across the island during the summer months. These open-air events offer a truly unique and unforgettable setting for music lovers, allowing visitors to take in the island's captivating natural landscapes while listening to the talents of both local and internationally renowned performers.

The Tynwald Hill Festival, held annually in July on the historic Tynwald Hill in the village of St. John's, is perhaps the most well-known of the Isle of Man's outdoor concert series. This event, which honors the island's ancient parliamentary traditions, features a diverse lineup of live music acts, including traditional Manx folk ensembles and contemporary rock and pop artists. For the best experience, arrive early to get a good spot on the hillside, bring a picnic basket and a cozy blanket, and soak up the lively atmosphere as the music echoes across the verdant Manx countryside.

Another must-see outdoor concert destination on the Isle of Man is the iconic Laxey Wheel, the world's largest working waterwheel, which provides a stunning backdrop for the annual Laxey Wheel Festival in August. Visitors can enjoy a diverse range of live music performances, from rousing Celtic folk tunes to energetic rock and roll, all while admiring the engineering marvel that is the Laxey Wheel and the picturesque Laxey Valley.

Aside from the island's outdoor concert offerings, the Isle of Man has a thriving network of live music venues that cater to a diverse range of musical tastes and styles. The Gaiety Theatre in Douglas, the island's capital city, stands out as a true crown jewel, with its magnificent Victorian-era architecture and world-class acoustics hosting a wide range of performances, from classical concerts and West End-style musicals to intimate folk and jazz showcases.

For a more intimate and immersive live music experience, we recommend stopping by one of the island's charming pubs and bars, many of which host regular live music nights with talented local and visiting musicians. The Mitre in Ramsey, the Centenary Centre in Peel, and the Erin Arts Centre in Port Erin are just a few of the island's popular venues where visitors can enjoy the island's musical talent while immersed in the convivial atmosphere of a traditional Manx watering hole.

Whether you prefer the grand scale of an outdoor concert or the intimate atmosphere of a pub performance, the Isle of Man's vibrant live music scene is sure to be a highlight of your Manx adventure. Plan your musical itinerary using the island's event calendars and visitor resources, and keep the spirit of discovery and delight in mind as you explore the island's diverse array of captivating live music experiences.

Sporting Events and Motorsports

While the Isle of Man's calendar of live music events and cultural festivals piques people's interest, the island also hosts a wide range of internationally recognized athletic events and motorsports competitions that are sure to excite tourists looking for a little more thrill.

The iconic Isle of Man TT (Tourist Trophy) Races, a legendary motorcycle racing festival that has enthralled fans since 1907, are the pinnacle of the island's sporting legacy. This exhilarating event, held every two weeks in June, draws legions of motorsports enthusiasts from all over the world to witness the sheer skill and bravery of the world's top motorcycle racers as they navigate the island's legendary 37.73-mile (60.72-kilometer) Mountain Course. For those who are fortunate enough to obtain tickets, the Isle of

Man TT promises an unforgettable experience, with the opportunity to immerse oneself in the event's electrifying atmosphere, explore interactive exhibits commemorating the race's illustrious history, and even take a guided tour of the iconic Snaefell Mountain Course to appreciate the full scope of this legendary racing circuit.

Aside from the Isle of Man TT, the island hosts a variety of other captivating sporting events, each of which provides visitors with a unique glimpse into the Manx people's deep-rooted desire for athletic excellence. The annual Isle of Man Sportive, for example, invites cyclists to put their skills to the test on a series of difficult road courses that showcase the island's breathtaking natural landscapes, whereas the Manx Mountain Marathon tests runners' endurance across the rugged terrain of the Manx hills and valleys.

For those who prefer more aquatic activities, the Isle of Man's calendar of sailing regattas and water sports competitions is equally impressive, with events such as the Peel Regatta and the Isle of Man Beach Games attracting participants and spectators from all over the globe. Whether you're admiring the precision and skill of the island's competitive sailors or participating in activities like stand-up paddleboarding and beach volleyball, these maritime-themed events are sure to leave an impression.

Of course, no discussion of the Isle of Man's sporting legacy would be complete unless it included the island's rich history in motocross and off-road racing. The annual Manx International Rally, for example, has captivated rally racing fans since the 1950s, with drivers navigating the island's difficult network of rural roads and tracks in pursuit of victory. Meanwhile, the Isle of Man Motocross Festival showcases the island's best off-road riders as they race their high-powered machines across a series of thrilling competitive courses.

Regardless of your athletic abilities, the Isle of Man's calendar of sporting events and motorsports competitions promises to provide an unforgettable experience that honors the island's rich heritage, natural beauty, and enduring spirit of adventure. Plan your itinerary using the island's comprehensive event listings and visitor resources, and don't forget to enjoy the thrill of the moment as you immerse yourself in the electrifying energy of these world-class sporting events.

Theaters, Cinemas, and Arts Venues

Immerse yourself in the rich artistic traditions and modern creative talents of the Manx people by visiting the island's thriving theater, cinema, and arts venue network. It's a must-do experience for anyone interested in learning more about the fascinating cultural tapestry of the Isle of Man.

The stunning Gaiety Theatre in Douglas, the island's capital city, is the focal point of the performing arts scene. Built as a true architectural and cultural gem, it has been mesmerizing audiences since its grand opening in 1899. With its superb acoustics and painstakingly restored auditorium, this magnificent theater from the Victorian era is the go-to venue for opera, classical music, and musical productions in the vein of West End shows. We strongly advise getting tickets to one of the Gaiety's well-known shows because of its superb programming and cozy atmosphere, which are sure to make an impression.

The Isle of Man has a delightful selection of independent movie theaters and art house cinemas that offer a welcome alternative to the multiplex experience for those who enjoy the arts of cinema. The Cinemas@Bucks movie theater complex in Douglas is a must-see location because of its cutting-edge screening rooms, varied programming, and welcoming, neighborhood-focused ambiance. A unique window into the island's rich cultural legacy is provided by the Centenary Centre cinema in the quaint town of Peel, which regularly hosts screenings of historic movies and documentaries that honor the history and customs of the Manx people.

The Isle of Man is home to a thriving network of art galleries and theaters that present the island's gifted local craftsmen and artists. This network extends beyond the realm of theater and film. The Manx Museum and National Art Gallery, located in the quaint village of Castletown, provide guests with a thorough overview of the island's rich artistic history through their permanent collections, which span centuries of Manx decorative arts, painting, and sculpture. Attending one of the museum's rotating temporary exhibitions, which frequently showcase the creations of modern Manx artists and craftspeople, could provide a more immersive experience.

The island's many arts and cultural institutions, like the Laxey Woollen Mill and the Erin Arts Centre in Port Erin, provide a plethora of workshops and classes that let guests interact directly with the centuries-old artistic traditions of the Manx people for those looking for a more hands-on creative experience. These enriching experiences, which range from learning the intricate techniques of Manx lace-making to trying your hand at traditional Gaelic storytelling, promise to infuse your Manx adventure with a deeper sense of personal connection and cultural appreciation.

To make sure you don't miss any of the must-see shows, exhibitions, or interactive experiences, consult the island's extensive event calendars and visitor resources as you organize your exploration of the vibrant arts and cultural scene on the Isle of Man. And never forget that your trip through the cultural tapestry of the Isle of Man is bound to be both educational and unique, whether you're taking in the opulence of the Gaiety Theatre or losing yourself in the intimate creative energy of a locals arts center.

CHAPTER 9.

ACCOMMODATION AND DINING

Hotels, Inns, and Guesthouses

As you plan your immersive journey through the enchanting Isle of Man, selecting the right accommodations can be the key to unlocking the full depth and breadth of the island's captivating charm. From grand historic hotels steeped in Manx heritage to cozy guesthouses that offer a warm, intimate escape, the Isle of Man boasts a diverse array of premier lodging options to suit every traveler's needs and preferences.

Grand Hotels Steeped in Manx Heritage

The Empress Hotel, located in the heart of Douglas, the Isle of Man's capital city, is a true icon of the island's illustrious history. This magnificent Victorian-era property, built in 1897, has long been a favorite among discerning travelers, providing an unrivaled combination of timeless elegance and modern comfort. Guests are greeted by the hotel's magnificent neoclassical façade and led into a world of refined sophistication, complete with meticulously restored public spaces that evoke the grandeur of bygone eras.

The Empress Hotel's 102 well-appointed guest rooms and suites feature plush furnishings, en-suite bathrooms, and a variety of modern amenities, ensuring a truly relaxing and rejuvenating stay. Aside from the impeccable accommodations, the hotel also has a renowned restaurant serving exquisite Manx-inspired cuisine, as well as a cozy lounge and bar area ideal for unwinding after a day of exploring. The Empress Hotel, located just steps from Douglas' picturesque promenade and the island's bustling central business district, is an ideal base for exploring the best of the Isle of Man. Rates at the Empress Hotel begin at £150 per night.

For those looking for a more intimate, historic hotel experience, the Milntown Hotel in Ramsey's charming northern town is an excellent option. This 12-room boutique property, housed in a beautifully preserved 18th-century manor house, provides guests with a fully immersive experience of the island's rich architectural and cultural heritage. Each guest room is uniquely decorated with period-inspired furnishings and antique accents, resulting in a warm, welcoming environment that transports guests back in time. Guests can enjoy the hotel's acclaimed on-site restaurant, which serves the best locally sourced Manx ingredients, or stroll through the property's expansive gardens and parklands, which include a charming café and artisanal shopping opportunities. With its tranquil countryside setting and easy access to the island's northern attractions, the Milntown Hotel is an enchanting home base for those looking for a truly authentic Manx experience. Prices at the Milntown Hotel begin at £120 per night.

Cozy Manx Inns Offer Warm Hospitality

For a more intimate and locally inspired lodging experience, the Isle of Man's network of traditional Manx inns is sure to please. One such gem is the Bradda Glen Inn, which sits atop the dramatic coastal cliffs of the island's stunning southern region. This family-owned establishment, which has been welcoming visitors since the nineteenth century, has 12 well-appointed guest rooms, each infused with charming Manx character and equipped with modern amenities. Guests can enjoy the inn's renowned restaurant, which serves only the best local seafood and produce, or explore the property's network of scenic walking trails that wind along the rugged Manx coastline. With its breathtaking ocean views and proximity to attractions such as the Cregneash Folk Village and the Calf of Man nature reserve, the Bradda Glen Inn is an ideal choice for those looking for a truly immersive Manx experience. The Bradda Glen Inn's rates start at £95 per night.

Further north, the Whitestone Hotel in the charming town of Peel is another shining example of the Isle of Man's well-known hospitality. This 18-room inn, housed in a beautifully restored Victorian-era building, combines modern amenities with the timeless charm of Manx tradition. Guests can expect well-appointed rooms, many of which have breathtaking views of Peel's iconic harbor and medieval castle, as well as the hotel's renowned restaurant, which serves delectable Manx-inspired cuisine in a cozy, convivial setting. Beyond the property, the Whitestone Hotel's central location makes it an excellent starting point for exploring Peel's many historic attractions and outdoor recreation opportunities. Rates at the Whitestone Hotel begin at £110 per night.

Charming Manx Guesthouses for a Warm, Intimate Escape
For travelers looking for a more personalized and intimate lodging experience, the Isle of Man's network of charming guesthouses is an excellent alternative to traditional hotels. One standout option is the Berkeley House in Port Erin, a picturesque coastal town.

This five-room property, housed in a beautifully restored Victorian-era villa, offers guests a cozy, home-away-from-home atmosphere, enhanced by impeccable service and attention to detail. Guests can expect well-appointed rooms, some with panoramic views of the Irish Sea, as well as a delicious daily breakfast featuring the best local and seasonal Manx ingredients. Beyond the property, the Berkeley House's central location makes it an excellent starting point for exploring the island's beautiful southern coastline and vibrant local culture. The Berkeley House's rates start at £90 per night.

Further north, in the charming seaside town of Ramsey, the Arrandale House & Gardens provides a truly unique and enchanting guesthouse experience. This elegant Edwardian-era property, set amidst lush, meticulously manicured gardens, has only six luxuriously appointed guest rooms, each infused with a soothing blend of historic charm and modern amenities. Guests can look forward to enjoying the guesthouse's well-known afternoon tea service, exploring the property's picturesque grounds, or simply relaxing in the inviting guest lounge. With its tranquil setting and easy access to Ramsey's many cultural and outdoor attractions, the Arrandale House & Gardens is an excellent choice for those looking for a relaxing and rejuvenating Manx getaway. The Arrandale House & Gardens offers rates starting at £120 per night.

The Glenlough Guest House in Douglas, the Isle of Man's capital, rounds out the island's guesthouse offerings. This charming six-room property, housed in a beautifully preserved Victorian-era townhouse, provides a warm and welcoming atmosphere just steps from Douglas' bustling promenade and central business district. Rooms are tastefully decorated with period-inspired furnishings and modern amenities, and the guesthouse's friendly hosts are always available to provide expert recommendations and assistance. Each morning, guests can enjoy a delicious homemade breakfast, preparing them for a day of exploring the island's many cultural and historic attractions. With its unrivaled location and dedication to personalized service, the Glenlough Guest House is an excellent choice for those looking for an authentic Manx guesthouse experience. The Glenlough Guest House offers rates starting at £80 per night.

Whether you choose to immerse yourself in the grand historic splendor of the Empress Hotel, the cozy charm of a traditional Manx inn, or the warm, intimate ambiance of a charming guesthouse, the Isle of Man's diverse array of accommodations promises to take your Manx adventure to new heights of comfort, authenticity, and unforgettable experience. To secure your preferred lodging option, consult the island's comprehensive visitor resources and book your stay ahead of time.

Self-Catering Cottages and Holiday Homes

For travelers seeking a truly immersive and independent experience on the enchanting Isle of Man, the island's diverse array of self-catering cottages and holiday homes offer the perfect blend of home comforts and unparalleled access to the Manx landscape and culture.

Cozy Coastal Cottages for a Serene Escape

Nestled along the island's rugged and breathtaking southern coastline, the Cregneash Cottages in the charming village of the same name offer an idyllic self-catering retreat for those seeking a peaceful and authentic Manx experience. These four lovingly restored 19th-century cottages, each sleeping up to six people, provide a glimpse into the island's rich cultural heritage, complete with traditional Manx architectural features and furnishings that evoke the island's historic pastoral way of life. Guests can expect well-equipped kitchens, cozy living areas with wood-burning stoves, and stunning views of the surrounding countryside and the distant Irish Sea. Beyond the cottage's amenities, visitors will be just a few steps away from the Cregneash Folk Village, a living museum showcasing the island's traditional way of life, as well as a network of scenic coastal walking trails that wind along the dramatic Manx cliffs. With rates starting at £150 per night, the Cregneash Cottages provide excellent value for those looking for a truly immersive Manx vacation.

The Bradda Glen Cottages in Port Erin, in the south, are an excellent choice for a more secluded and serene self-catering experience. These three charming holiday homes, each sleeping up to four people, are nestled among the rugged coastal landscapes of the Manx countryside, offering a true sense of tranquillity and privacy. Guests can expect well-appointed interiors with fully equipped kitchens, cozy living areas, and breathtaking views of the surrounding countryside and dramatic cliffs. Beyond the cottages, visitors will have easy access to the island's stunning coastal walking trails, as well as the charming seaside town of Port Erin, which has a variety of local shops, restaurants, and historic attractions. With rates starting at £130 per night, the Bradda Glen Cottages provide an ideal home base for those looking to immerse themselves in the Isle of Man's breathtaking natural beauty.

Historic Manx Farmhouses offer a glimpse into island life.
The historic Thie Reagh Farmhouse in Ramsey, the Isle of Man's northern town, is an excellent choice for a truly unique self-catering experience that honors the island's rich agricultural heritage. This beautifully restored 18th-century property, which can accommodate up to eight guests, allows visitors to step back in time and experience the island's pastoral way of life. Guests can expect charming period-inspired furnishings, a fully equipped kitchen for preparing homemade Manx meals, and cozy living areas that promote relaxation and rejuvenation. Beyond the farmhouse's amenities, visitors will have easy access to the island's

network of scenic walking trails, as well as the vibrant town of Ramsey, which boasts a plethora of local shops, cafes, and historic attractions. With rates beginning at £180 per night, the Thie Reagh Farmhouse is an excellent value for those looking for an authentic and immersive Manx experience.

Further south, in the picturesque coastal village of Niarbyl, the Ballacreggan Farmhouse provides another exceptional self-catering option for those looking to fully embrace the Isle of Man's rural charm. This lovingly restored 19th-century property, which can sleep up to six people, has traditional Manx architectural details, a fully equipped modern kitchen, and cozy living areas that open out onto sweeping views of the surrounding countryside and dramatic coastline. Guests can enjoy exploring the farmhouse's expansive grounds, which include scenic walking trails and a private beach access point, as well as the nearby Niarbyl Heritage Trail, which provides a fascinating look into the island's geological and cultural history. With rates starting at £200 per night, the Ballacreggan Farmhouse is an excellent choice for those looking for a truly unique and immersive Manx experience.

Urban Oases: Stylish Holiday Homes in Douglas.

For travelers looking for a self-catering experience that combines the conveniences of modern life with easy access to the Isle of Man's vibrant cultural attractions, the island's capital city of Douglas has a plethora of exceptional holiday home options.

The Strand Apartments are a standout choice, with a collection of stylishly appointed studio and one-bedroom units just steps from Douglas' picturesque promenade and bustling central business district. These modern holiday homes, which can accommodate two to four guests, have fully equipped kitchens, comfortable living areas, and private balconies or terraces with panoramic views of the Irish Sea. Guests can enjoy the convenience of being within walking distance of Douglas' numerous restaurants, shops, and cultural institutions, as well as the privacy and independence of self-catering accommodations. With rates starting at £120 per night, the Strand Apartments are an excellent value for those looking for an urban Manx adventure.

Further inland, the Ridgeway Townhouse Apartments in Douglas offer another appealing self-catering option for those looking for a sophisticated, centrally located home base. These elegantly appointed one and two-bedroom units, which can accommodate two to four guests, include stylish modern furnishings, fully equipped kitchens, and cozy living areas that evoke the island's historic architecture. Guests can look forward to being just a short walk from Douglas' bustling promenade and the city's many cultural attractions, including the iconic Gaiety Theatre and the Manx Museum. With rates starting at £150 per night, the Ridgeway Townhouse Apartments provide an exceptional combination of comfort, convenience, and Manx-inspired style.

Whether you prefer the tranquil coastal charm of a Manx cottage, the historic rural ambiance of a traditional farmhouse, or the urban sophistication of a Douglas-based holiday home, the Isle of Man's diverse array of self-catering accommodations will provide the ideal home base for your Manx adventure. To secure your ideal self-catering escape, consult the island's comprehensive visitor resources and book your preferred property ahead of time.

Unique Dining Experiences and Local Cuisine

Be ready to embark on a gastronomic adventure that honors the island's rich agricultural legacy, varied cultural influences, and close connection to the bounty of the surrounding seas as you explore the enchanted Isle of Man. The Isle of Man's thriving dining scene promises to delight and tantalize the senses, offering visitors a true taste of the island's distinct gastronomic identity. Dishes range from inventive, locally-inspired dishes to traditional Manx delicacies.

Manx Kippers: A Beloved Seafood Staple

No visit to the Isle of Man is complete without trying the island's famous smoked kippers, a beloved seafood delicacy that has been a staple of Manx cuisine for centuries. According to local fisherman John Corkill, "Our kippers are simply the best anywhere in the world. We take great pride in the time-honored methods we use to smoke and cure these exquisite herring, ensuring that they retain their rich, buttery flavor and firm, flaky texture." Visitors can enjoy the iconic Manx kipper at a variety of local establishments, including the charming Harbour Lights Café in Peel, where the fish is served with traditional Manx potatoes and Laxey keeill bread, and the award-winning Michelin-starred Number 16 restaurant in Douglas, where the kippers are showcased in innovative preparations that highlight their exceptional quality.

Laxey Loaghtan Lamb: A Celebration of Manx Terroir.

The Isle of Man's rugged landscapes and mild maritime climate have long encouraged the production of high-quality lamb, with the Laxey Loaghtan breed standing out as a true source of Manx pride. "Our Laxey Loaghtan lambs graze on the nutrient-rich grasses and heather of the island's glens and hills, imparting a unique, earthy flavor that you simply can't find anywhere else," Sarah Corlett, a farmer from Ramsey, says. Visitors can enjoy the distinct flavor of Laxey Loaghtan lamb at establishments such as the Milntown Hotel in Ramsey, where the meat is featured in a variety of traditional Manx preparations, and the Erin Arts Centre in Port Erin, where the lamb is highlighted in a seasonal tasting menu that celebrates the island's exceptional local produce.

Queenies: The Isle of Man's Prized Scallop.

One of the true jewels of Manx cuisine is the island's renowned queenies, or queen scallops, which are harvested from the nutrient-rich waters that surround the Isle of Man. "Our queenies are simply unparalleled in terms of their sweetness, tenderness, and overall quality," says Peel-based seafood purveyor Michael Quayle. "The cool, pristine waters of the Irish Sea, combined with our sustainable fishing practices, allow us to produce a scallop that is truly in a league of its own." Visitors can enjoy the exceptional flavor of Manx queenies at restaurants such as The Sidings Restaurant in Douglas, where the scallops are served in a variety of creative preparations, and the Bradda Glen Inn in Port Erin, where they are showcased in a classic, lightly seared presentation that allows their natural sweetness to shine through.

Manx Cheddar, A Cheesemaker's Delight

The Isle of Man's rich agricultural heritage has also resulted in an exceptional selection of artisanal cheeses, with Manx Cheddar standing out as a genuine source of local pride. "Our Manx Cheddar is the result of generations of cheesemaking expertise, combined with the unique terroir of the Isle of Man," explains Castletown-based cheesemaker Emma Corlett. "The creamy, full-bodied flavor and firm, slightly crumbly texture of our cheddar is a direct reflection of the lush pastures and cool, maritime climate that our dairy cows call home." Visitors can savor the exceptional quality of Manx Cheddar at establishments such as The Tynwald Mill in St. John's, where the cheese is featured in a variety of creative dishes and platters, and the Laxey Woollen Mill, where it is available for purchase alongside other artisanal Manx products.

Manx Kale and Potatoes: Celebrating Island Bounty.
Manx cuisine is based on a deep appreciation for the island's exceptional agricultural bounty, with locally grown kale and potatoes being two of the most celebrated and versatile ingredients. "Our Manx kale and potatoes are the foundation of so many of our traditional dishes, from hearty stews to comforting shepherd's pies," says Douglas-based chef Liam Quine. "The cool, maritime climate and nutrient-rich soil of the Isle of Man allows these humble ingredients to flourish, imparting a depth of flavor and texture that you simply can't find anywhere else." Visitors can enjoy the exceptional quality of Manx kale and potatoes at restaurants such as The Gaiety Theatre in Douglas, where they are featured in a traditional Manx 'bunshen' supper, and the Bradda Glen Inn in Port Erin, where they are highlighted in a variety of innovative preparations that celebrate the island's culinary traditions.

Manx Ale and Cider: A Fresh Taste of the Isle
No tour of the Isle of Man's dining scene would be complete without trying the island's exceptional selection of locally produced ales and ciders. "Our Manx ales and ciders are a true reflection of the island's rich agricultural heritage and independent spirit," says Ramsey-based brewer Matthew Quirk. "From the crisp, refreshing taste of our Bushy's Golden Wonders

to the robust, complex flavors of our Okell's beers, each sip transports you to the heart of the Isle of Man." Visitors can explore the breadth of the island's craft beverage offerings at places such as The Mitre in Ramsey, which has a large selection of Manx ales and ciders on tap, and the Centenary Centre in Peel, where they can sample a variety of local brews while listening to live music and cultural performances.

Manx seafood chowder is a comforting coastal classic.

As an island nation, the Isle of Man's culinary traditions are deeply rooted in the bounty of the surrounding seas, with the island's famous seafood chowder standing out as a quintessential Manx comfort dish. "Our seafood chowder is a true celebration of the Isle of Man's maritime heritage," says Port Erin chef Emma Quayle. "We start with a rich, creamy broth that's infused with the flavors of local produce like Manx kale and potatoes, then we add a generous selection of the finest seafood the Irish Sea has to offer - queenies, langoustines, and more." Visitors can enjoy the comforting warmth and exceptional quality of Manx seafood chowder at restaurants such as The Harbour Lights Café in Peel and the Erin Arts Centre in Port Erin, where it is frequently featured as a seasonal specialty.

Manx Fudge and Ice Cream: Sweet Indulgence

No visit to the Isle of Man is complete without sampling the island's exceptional homemade fudge and ice cream. "Our Manx fudge and ice cream are the result of generations of confectionery and creamery expertise, combined with the finest local ingredients," explains Sarah Quayle, a confectioner from Douglas. "From the rich, creamy texture of our vanilla ice cream to the decadent, buttery goodness of our sea salt fudge, every bite is a true taste of the Isle of Man." Visitors can enjoy these sweet Manx delicacies at a number of local establishments, including the Laxey Woollen Mill, where the fudge and ice cream are displayed alongside other artisanal Manx products, and the Milntown Hotel in Ramsey, where they are frequently featured as part of the property's acclaimed afternoon tea service.

Whether you're savoring the exceptional quality of Manx kippers and queenies, indulging in the hearty comfort of Manx kale and potatoes, or enjoying the island's exceptional selection of craft beverages and confections, the Isle of Man's vibrant dining scene is sure to leave an indelible mark on your palate and memory. To plan your culinary adventure, consult the island's comprehensive visitor resources, and don't be afraid to interact with local chefs, producers, and purveyors to gain a better understanding of the distinct flavors and traditions that define the Isle of Man's exceptional gastronomic identity.

Vegetarian and Vegan Options

As the Isle of Man continues to evolve and embrace sustainable, plant-based lifestyles, the island's dining scene has similarly blossomed, offering a diverse array of exceptional vegetarian and vegan options that cater to the discerning tastes of health-conscious and eco-minded travelers.

Manx Produce Reimagined: Vegetarian Delights at The Shire

The Shire, a charming restaurant in Douglas, the Isle of Man's capital city, is at the forefront of the island's vegetarian dining scene, with a reputation for innovative, plant-based interpretations of traditional Manx cuisine. "We believe that the exceptional produce cultivated right here on the Isle of Man has the power to shine on its own, without the need for meat or dairy," says owner and head chef Liam Corlett. "Our mission is to celebrate the island's bountiful agricultural heritage through dishes that are not only delicious, but also sustainable and nourishing." The "Manx Meadow" salad, which features a vibrant array of locally grown greens, vegetables, and edible flowers, and the "Laxey Loaghtan Lentil Shepherd's Pie," a hearty, plant-based twist on a Manx classic, are two standout menu items. The Shire, with its commitment to sourcing the best local, organic ingredients and its cozy, welcoming ambiance, has become a must-see destination for vegetarian and vegan travelers looking to immerse themselves in the Isle of Man's exceptional plant-based culinary culture.

Coastal Sanctuary: Vegan Dining at The Beach Hut.

Tucked away in the picturesque coastal village of Port Erin, The Beach Hut has emerged as a shining beacon for those looking for exceptional vegan dining experiences amidst the Isle of Man's breathtaking natural landscapes. "Our mission is to create a sanctuary for plant-based diners, where they can savor the bounty of the island's fertile land and pristine seas in a serene, oceanfront setting," says Emma Quayle, the restaurant's chef.

The Beach Hut's menu celebrates local, seasonal produce, with standout dishes like the "Manx Kale and Quinoa Bowl," which features a nutrient-dense blend of island-grown greens, ancient grains, and vibrant vegetable toppings, and the "Queenies and Chips," a vegan interpretation of the island's renowned scallop dish, made with sustainably sourced, plant-based seafood alternatives. Beyond its impressive culinary offerings, The Beach Hut is committed to environmental stewardship, using renewable energy sources and implementing a zero-waste policy to solidify its reputation as a true sanctuary for conscious, plant-based travelers.

Conscious Comfort at The Manx Vegan.

For a truly immersive vegetarian and vegan dining experience that captures the essence of Manx hospitality, The Manx Vegan in Ramsey, in the north, is an excellent choice. "We believe that plant-based cuisine can, and should, be just as comforting, satisfying, and downright delicious as traditional Manx fare," says co-owner and head chef Sarah Corlett. "Our mission is to reimagine the island's beloved dishes through a vegetarian and vegan lens, while also highlighting the incredible bounty of local produce that the Isle of Man has to offer." Standout menu items include the "Laxey Loaghtan Lentil Shepherd's Pie," a hearty, plant-based take on a Manx classic, and the "Queenies and Chips," which features a sustainable, plant-based seafood alternative that captures the flavor and texture of the island's renowned scallops. Beyond its exceptional cuisine, The Manx Vegan has a cozy, convivial atmosphere and a commitment to sustainability that appeals to eco-conscious visitors looking for an authentic, Manx-inspired dining experience.

The Cutting Edge of Vegetarian Dining: Promenade

For a truly innovative and elevated vegetarian dining experience, Promenade in Douglas has emerged as a must-see destination for discerning plant-based travelers. "Our mission is to push the boundaries of what vegetarian cuisine can be, by continuously exploring new techniques, flavors, and presentations that showcase the exceptional quality and versatility of local, seasonal produce," Liam Quine, the head chef, states. Menu highlights include the "Manx Kale and Quinoa Risotto," a creamy, comforting dish infused with the distinct flavors of the island's nutrient-dense kale, and the "Manx Cheddar and Potato Terrine," a sophisticated, plant-based interpretation of a Manx classic that highlights the exceptional quality of the island's renowned artisanal cheese. With its sleek, modern ambiance and unwavering commitment to sustainability and innovation, Promenade has established itself as a dining destination that truly celebrates the Isle of Man's plant-based culinary potential.

Whether you're looking for a cozy, comfort-driven vegetarian experience that honors the island's rich Manx heritage, a plant-based sanctuary that highlights the exceptional bounty of the Isle of Man's coastal landscapes, or a cutting-edge, fine-dining vegetarian adventure that pushes the boundaries of culinary creativity, the Isle of Man's diverse array of vegetarian and vegan dining options promises to delight and inspire eco-conscious travelers from all over the world. Consult the island's extensive visitor resources to plan your plant-based culinary adventure and immerse yourself in the Isle of Man's thriving, sustainable food culture.

CHAPTER 10.

TIPS FOR VISITING THE ISLE OF MAN

Essential Travel Information and Resources

Getting to the Isle of Man

The Isle of Man is accessible via air and sea. Regular flights operate from various UK airports, including London, Manchester, and Liverpool, with journey times around 1 hour. Sea travel options include the Isle of Man Steam Packet Company, which operates daily ferry services from Heysham, Liverpool, and Dublin, with journey times ranging from 2-4 hours. The Isle of Man has its own international airport, located just outside of the capital, Douglas, offering convenient access for air travelers.

Getting Around the Isle of Man

The Isle of Man has a comprehensive public transportation network that includes buses, trains, and a heritage steam railway, allowing visitors to explore the island without a private vehicle. For those who prefer greater independence, rental cars are available from a variety of providers at the airport and in major cities. The island is also very pedestrian and cyclist friendly, with a network of scenic walking trails and designated bike lanes, making it simple to explore on foot or by bike.

Accommodation Options:

The Isle of Man has a wide variety of accommodation options, ranging from charming self-catering cottages and holiday homes to traditional bed and breakfasts, hotels, and luxury resorts. Visitors are encouraged to book their accommodations in advance, especially during peak travel seasons, to ensure the best availability and rates. Many accommodation providers on the Isle of Man are dedicated to sustainability and environmental stewardship, providing environmentally friendly amenities and practices.

Visitor Information and Resources

The Isle of Man's official tourism website (www.visitisleofman.com) is an invaluable resource for trip planning, with detailed information on attractions, events, dining, and more. Visitor information centers in Douglas, Peel, and other major towns can provide additional information, maps, and brochures to help you make the most of your Isle of Man visit. Social media channels, such as the Isle of Man's official Facebook, Twitter, and Instagram pages, are also excellent sources of current information, local insights, and inspiration.

Currency and Payment

The official currency of the Isle of Man is the Manx pound, which is equivalent to the British pound sterling. Most businesses accept major credit and debit cards, but it's a good idea to keep cash on hand for smaller transactions and local vendors. It is important to note that the Isle of Man is not part of the United Kingdom, so using your UK bank cards on the island may result in additional fees or charges. It is recommended that you check with your financial institution before traveling.

Travel Insurance and Health Considerations

Visitors to the Isle of Man are advised to purchase comprehensive travel insurance to cover unforeseen circumstances such as trip cancellations, medical emergencies, or lost/stolen belongings. The Isle of Man's healthcare system is well-developed, and visitors from the United Kingdom, the European Union, and some other countries may be eligible for free or reduced-cost medical care. It is recommended that you check your eligibility and obtain all necessary documentation prior to your trip. Those with specific medical conditions or dietary requirements should research the availability of specialized services or products on the island and make plans accordingly.

By becoming acquainted with this essential travel information and resources, you will be well-prepared to plan and enjoy a smooth and memorable visit to the enchanting Isle of Man.

Budgeting and Cost-Saving Strategies

Traveling to the Isle of Man can be an incredibly rewarding experience, but it's important to plan your budget carefully to ensure a smooth and financially responsible trip. By implementing some strategic cost-saving measures, you can make the most of your time on the island while keeping your expenses in check.

Accommodation: One of the most significant expenses for most travelers is their choice of lodging. To save money on lodging, look into self-catering holiday cottages, hostels, or camping/caravan sites, which can be significantly cheaper than traditional hotels. Furthermore, booking your accommodations well in advance or during the off season can often result in lower rates.

Transportation: The Isle of Man has a well-developed public transportation network that includes buses, trains, and the heritage steam railway. Using these inexpensive options can be an excellent way to explore the island without incurring the additional cost of renting a car. If you decide to rent a car, make sure to research and compare rates from various providers to find the best deal.

Dining: Although the Isle of Man is known for its excellent local cuisine, eating out every day can quickly deplete your budget. To balance your dining experiences, consider preparing some meals yourself, using the facilities in your hotel, or looking for low-cost restaurants and market stalls. Many establishments also offer special deals, such as set menus or early bird specials, to help you save money on your meals.

Attractions and Activities: The Isle of Man has a wealth of natural and cultural attractions, many of which are free or inexpensive to visit. Take advantage of these opportunities by tailoring your itinerary to the island's numerous parks, beaches, and heritage sites. Consider purchasing a Manx Explorer Pass, which provides discounted admission to multiple attractions, or exploring the island's network of scenic walking and cycling trails, which are completely free to use.

Souvenirs and Gifts: While it's tempting to indulge in the Isle of Man's exceptional selection of local products and crafts, keep your souvenir spending under control. Seek out local markets, craft fairs, and independent shops, which frequently offer lower prices than tourist-heavy areas. Consider purchasing nonperishable food items like Manx cheese, fudge, or preserves as inexpensive gifts and mementos.

Using these money-saving strategies, you can enjoy everything the Isle of Man has to offer without breaking the bank. Remember to do your research and plan ahead of time, and be willing to take advantage of the island's many free and low-cost activities. With some strategic budgeting, you can plan an unforgettable and financially responsible trip to this enchanting destination.

Responsible Tourism and Environmental Considerations

As an island known for its stunning natural beauty and rich environmental heritage, the Isle of Man has firmly established itself as a leader in sustainable tourism practices. Visitors to the island are encouraged to embrace a mindset of responsible travel, ensuring that their experiences contribute positively to the island's delicate ecosystems and local communities.

Environmental Stewardship: The Isle of Man has made significant strides toward environmental protection and conservation. From ambitious renewable energy targets to comprehensive waste management initiatives, the island has set the standard for sustainable tourism practices. Visitors are encouraged to support these efforts by conserving energy and water, properly disposing of waste, and choosing environmentally friendly modes of transportation such as public transportation, cycling, or walking.

Protecting Natural Habitats: The Isle of Man's diverse natural habitats, which include rugged coastlines, lush glens, and rolling hills, support a diverse range of flora and fauna. Visitors can help preserve these fragile ecosystems by following designated trails, not disturbing wildlife, and respecting the island's various conservation areas and nature reserves.

Supporting Local Businesses: By patronizing local businesses and purchasing locally sourced products, visitors can directly contribute to the island's economic well-being. From dining at independent restaurants featuring Manx-grown ingredients to shopping at artisanal markets and craft studios, these conscious choices contribute to the island's thriving network of sustainable, locally-owned businesses.

Cultural Preservation: The Isle of Man's rich cultural heritage, including its distinctive language, traditions, and art forms, is an essential component of the island's identity. Visitors can interact respectfully with these cultural elements by attending local festivals, workshops, and performances, as well as learning about the island's history and customs from knowledgeable residents.

Responsible Adventure: The Isle of Man's extensive network of outdoor recreational opportunities, including hiking, cycling, water sports, and birdwatching, offers limitless opportunities for exploration and adventure. Visitors are encouraged to approach these activities with a sense of responsible stewardship, adhering to Leave No Trace principles, respecting any access restrictions, and contributing to local conservation efforts.

Visitors to the Isle of Man can help to ensure that their experiences contribute positively to the island's long-term sustainability by adopting responsible tourism principles, as well as deepening their connection to the island's rich environmental and cultural heritage. Travelers can leave the Isle of Man better than they found it by making mindful choices and committing to sustainable practices, ensuring that future generations can enjoy its breathtaking natural wonders.

Manx Customs, Etiquette, and Local Lingo

Immersing yourself in the unique cultural fabric of the Isle of Man is an integral part of any truly memorable visit. By familiarizing yourself with the island's customs, etiquette, and local lingo, you can engage with the Manx people and their traditions in a more meaningful and respectful manner, ensuring a richer and more authentic experience.

Manx Customs and Etiquette:
Greetings: A warm "hello" (or "cashtal" in Manx Gaelic) and a friendly smile are universally appreciated by the Manx people. Handshakes are common, but avoid overly formal or stiff greetings.

Dress code: Casual and comfortable attire is generally the norm, especially in more rural or outdoor settings. However, some establishments, particularly upscale restaurants or formal events, may have slightly higher dress expectations.

Dining: Manx dining etiquette is relatively relaxed, with an emphasis on enjoying the food and company. It's generally acceptable to start eating when your meal is served, rather than waiting for everyone to be served.

Tipping: Tipping is not as ingrained in Manx culture as it is in some other countries. A 10% tip for exceptional service is considered generous, but is not always expected.

Punctuality: While Manx people are generally punctual, a slight delay is often forgiven, particularly for informal gatherings or social events.

Manx Lingo and Linguistic Nuances:

Manx Gaelic: The Manx language, a Celtic language closely related to Irish and Scottish Gaelic, was once nearly extinct but has undergone a remarkable revitalization in recent decades. While English is the primary language spoken, incorporating a few Manx words or phrases can be a delightful way to connect with the local culture.

Common Manx Expressions:
- "Gura mie ayd" (thank you)
- "Kys t'ou?" (how are you?)
- "Traa dy liooar" (time enough)
- "Moghrey mie" (good morning)
- "Fastyr mie" (good afternoon)
- "Oie vie" (good night)
- "Jees" (two)

- "Tree" (three)
- "Kiare" (four)
- "Queig" (five)
- "Shey" (six)

Manx Accents and Dialects: The Isle of Man has a wide variety of regional accents and dialects, each with its own distinct inflections and colloquialisms. For example, the Douglas accent, spoken in the island's capital, differs from the more rural accents heard in Peel and Ramsey. These linguistic variations may take some time to adjust to, but accepting them can enhance the richness of your cultural immersion.

By becoming familiar with these aspects of Manx culture, you will be able to confidently navigate the island's customs and etiquette, as well as interact with the locals in a more meaningful and respectful manner. This cultural awareness not only improves your travel experience, but also demonstrates your appreciation for the Manx way of life, which strengthens the bonds you form during your stay on this enchanting island.

CHAPTER 11.

5 DAYS IN THE ISLE OF MAN: THE ULTIMATE ITINERARY FOR FIRST TIME VISITORS.

Day 1: Exploring the Capital City of Douglas

Begin your Isle of Man adventure by immersing yourself in the vibrant energy of the island's capital, Douglas. As the economic and cultural heart of the island, this coastal city offers a wealth of captivating experiences to kickstart your 5-day journey.

Begin your day at the Manx Museum, a veritable treasure trove of the island's rich history and culture. Explore the engaging exhibits, which detail the Manx people's deep ties to the land, their maritime traditions, and the island's unique political and social dynamics over time. Explore the museum's extensive collection of Manx Gaelic artifacts, artwork, and historical documents to gain a better understanding of the island's cultural heritage. Plan to spend at least 1-2 hours exploring the museum's fascinating exhibits and interactive installations.

After a hearty Manx breakfast, go for a leisurely stroll along the iconic Douglas Promenade, a picturesque seafront esplanade lined with Victorian-era architecture and bustling with local activity. Admire the breathtaking views of Douglas Bay and the Irish Sea, then browse the charming shops, cafés, and eateries that line the promenade. This is an excellent location to soak up the island's relaxed seaside atmosphere and mingle with the friendly locals.

Next, visit the Manx Transport Museum to learn about the island's unique transportation history. The museum is housed in a beautifully restored Victorian building and features an impressive collection of vintage vehicles, including classic cars, motorcycles, and the iconic Manx Electric Railway carriages. Learn about the island's innovative engineering feats and how transportation has shaped the Manx way of life. Spend 1-2 hours exploring the museum's interesting exhibits and interactive displays.

For a truly Manx experience, stop by one of the city's charming cafés or tearooms for a traditional afternoon tea. Enjoy a variety of delicious Manx-inspired pastries, scones, and finger sandwiches, accompanied by a steaming pot of fragrant Manx tea. This leisurely interlude will be the perfect break from your morning explorations, allowing you to fully immerse yourself in the island's refined culinary heritage.

As the sun begins to set, head to the Gaiety Theatre, a beautifully restored Edwardian-era performance space that hosts a wide range of theatrical productions, concerts, and other cultural events. Check out the theater's schedule and get tickets to an evening show that interests you, whether it's a lively musical, a thought-provoking drama, or a captivating dance performance. Witnessing the island's vibrant performing arts scene will be an appropriate way to end your first day on the Isle of Man.

Consider staying at one of Douglas' well-appointed hotels or bed and breakfasts, such as the luxurious Empress Hotel (from £150 per night) or the charming Sefton Hotel (from £100 per night). These centrally located establishments will provide you with easy access to the city's attractions as well as a comfortable base to recharge for your upcoming adventures.

On your first day, immerse yourself in Douglas' rich history, cultural traditions, and lively atmosphere. This will lay the groundwork for a truly immersive and memorable exploration of the Isle of Man. This itinerary, which includes museum visits, scenic walks, culinary delights, and cultural performances, will help you make the most of your time in the island's vibrant capital.

Day 2: Discovering the Island's Natural Wonders

After a restful night in Douglas, embark on a journey to explore the Isle of Man's stunning natural landscapes on your second day.

Begin your day with a scenic hike through the picturesque Laxey Glen, a lush, wooded valley nestled in the island's central region. As you meander along the well-marked trails, take in the captivating sights and sounds of the Laxey River, which winds its way through the glen, forming a series of picturesque waterfalls and cascades. Keep an eye out for the diverse array of flora and fauna that thrive in this protected natural environment, from delicate wildflowers to the island's native birds and wildlife. Plan to spend 1-2 hours immersed in the tranquil beauty of Laxey Glen.

Next, head to the nearby town of Laxey, which is home to one of the island's most iconic landmarks, the Laxey Wheel. Also known as "Lady Isabella," this massive 72.5-foot water wheel is the world's largest working waterwheel and was once an important part of the island's thriving mining industry. Take a guided tour of the wheel and its surrounding buildings, learning about the incredible engineering feats that enabled this marvel. After that, stroll through Laxey's charming streets, stopping at local shops and cafés to learn more about the town's fascinating history and culture. Plan on spending 1-2 hours at the Laxey Wheel and exploring the surroundings.

Continue your journey west to the rugged Calf of Man, a small island that serves as a popular nature reserve. To reach this remote gem, take a boat tour or walk the scenic coastal path. You'll be able to see a variety of seabirds, including puffins, cormorants, and kittiwakes, as well as the island's resident grey seals. Spend time exploring the Calf's dramatic cliffs, boulder-strewn beaches, and ancient historical sites, while admiring the breathtaking views of the surrounding Irish Sea. Allow 2-3 hours for your visit to the Calf of Man.

Peel Castle

As lunchtime approaches, head to the charming seaside town of Peel, which is known for its fresh, locally sourced seafood. Enjoy a delicious meal at one of the town's waterfront restaurants, such as the Trafalgar Hotel's renowned seafood bistro, where you can savor the flavors of the island's abundant maritime resources. After lunch, visit Peel Castle, a well-preserved medieval fortress perched atop a rocky headland, and stroll through the historic Peel Harbor, taking in the quaint atmosphere of this quintessential Manx fishing town.

As the day winds down, take a scenic drive back to Douglas, admiring the stunning coastal landscapes and rolling hills that define the island's natural beauty. This evening, you may want to eat at one of the city's well-known restaurants, such as The Shore, which celebrates the island's exceptional local produce and culinary traditions.

Consider booking a room at a charming bed and breakfast or self-catering cottage in the Laxey or Peel areas to fully immerse yourself in the island's picturesque countryside and coastal scenery. Some recommended options include the Ballacregga Corn Mill in Laxey (starting at £90 per night) and the Peel Bay Apartments in Peel (beginning at £120 per night).

Spending your second day exploring the Isle of Man's breathtaking natural landscapes will give you a greater appreciation for the island's rugged beauty and its residents' enduring connection to the land. From the tranquil glens and cascading waterfalls to the dramatic coastal cliffs and thriving wildlife habitats, this itinerary will leave you with a deep appreciation for the island's environmental treasures.

Day 3: Immersing in Manx Heritage and Traditions

On your third day on the Isle of Man, immerse yourself in the island's rich cultural heritage and traditional practices, gaining a deeper understanding of the Manx people's unique identity and way of life.

Begin your day with a visit to the Tynwald, the world's oldest continuous parliamentary institution. Witness the annual Tynwald Day ceremony, a centuries-old tradition where the island's government convenes in an open-air setting to enact laws and celebrate the island's autonomy. Observe the procession of dignitaries, listen to the formal readings, and soak in the atmosphere of this unique political and cultural event. Plan to spend 1-2 hours at the Tynwald ceremony, allowing ample time to explore the surrounding area and learn more about the island's governmental structures and traditions.

Next, visit the tranquil Manx National Glens, a network of picturesque valleys and forests that provide a peaceful escape from the bustling towns. Hike through the lush, tree-lined landscapes, soaking up the sights and sounds of the island's diverse flora and fauna. Along the way, take in the geological wonders that have shaped the Manx landscape, from dramatic rock formations to tranquil streams and waterfalls. This immersion in the island's natural heritage will provide a better understanding of the Manx people's strong bond with the land. Allow 2-3 hours for your exploration of the Manx National Glens.

In the afternoon, attend a hands-on workshop to learn about the island's rich culinary and artistic traditions. Choose from a variety of options, including a Manx cooking class where you'll learn how to make traditional Manx dishes with locally sourced ingredients and a Manx craft workshop where you can make your own Manx tartan, pottery, or other artisanal keepsakes. These interactive experiences will not only teach you new skills, but will also give you a better understanding of the Manx people's cultural heritage and the island's vibrant creative community. Plan on spending 2-3 hours completely immersed in your chosen workshop.

To round out your day, take a guided tour of a local brewery or distillery, where you'll be able to sample the island's famous artisanal spirits. Learn about the Manx people's long-standing distilling and brewing traditions, as well as the unique methods and ingredients that give these beverages their distinct flavors. Whether you take a tour of the Isle of Man Distillery or the Bushy's Brewery, you'll leave with a greater appreciation for the island's artisanal spirit-making heritage. Allow 1-2 hours for your brewery or distillery visit.

In the evening, attend a traditional Manx music and dance performance to immerse yourself in the island's vibrant cultural traditions. These captivating events are frequently held at venues such as the Gaiety Theatre and the Centenary Centre, highlighting the island's rich musical heritage as well as the enduring passion of its talented performers. This cultural experience will be the ideal way to cap off a day of deep immersion in the Manx way of life.

Consider staying at a charming country inn or a quaint self-catering cottage in the heart of the Manx countryside, such as Ard-Ane Country House (starting at £120 per night) or Thie-ny-Lheeaney Cottages (starting at £150 per night). These accommodations will provide you with a peaceful retreat while also allowing you to connect with the island's rural character.

By spending your third day exploring the Manx people's cultural heritage, traditions, and artisanal crafts, you'll gain a deep appreciation for the island's distinct identity and the enduring spirit of its residents. This immersive experience will broaden your knowledge of the Isle of Man and leave you with a lasting connection to its fascinating cultural tapestry.

Day 4: Experiencing the Isle of Man's Outdoor Pursuits

On your fourth day on the Isle of Man, immerse yourself in the island's vast array of outdoor recreational opportunities, allowing you to fully appreciate the breathtaking natural landscapes from a variety of perspectives.

Begin your day with a nostalgic journey aboard the Isle of Man Steam Railway, one of the island's most iconic modes of transportation. Board the lovingly restored Victorian-era carriages and enjoy a leisurely ride through the picturesque Manx countryside, taking in the rolling hills, charming villages, and stunning vistas that unfold before you. This historical railway experience will transport you back in time and provide a unique vantage point from which to admire the island's natural beauty. Plan to allocate 1-2 hours for your steam railway adventure.

Beautiful coast of the Isle of Man from Peel Hill in Peel

After disembarking, put on your hiking boots and explore the island's vast network of walking trails. Consider taking on a section of the Coastal Path, which highlights the dramatic cliffs, secluded bays, and rugged headlands that define the Manx coastline. Alternatively, take a hike along the Millennium Way, a long-distance trail that runs through the island's interior, providing panoramic views of the rolling hills, forests, and moorlands. Whatever trail you take, be prepared to be immersed in the island's breathtaking natural landscapes and connect with the island's rich environmental heritage. Plan to hike for 2-3 hours, depending on the trail and your fitness level.

Spend the afternoon trying out a water-based activity like kayaking, stand-up paddleboarding, or sailing to get a new perspective on the island's coastal wonders. Several local operators, including Explore Isle of Man and Island Outdoor, provide guided tours and equipment rentals, allowing you to explore the island's hidden coves, sea caves, and wildlife-rich marine environments from the water. This intimate encounter with the island's coastal landscapes will leave you with a renewed appreciation for Manx maritime heritage. Plan to spend 2-3 hours on your water-based adventure.

As the day comes to a close, visit the Curraghs Wildlife Park, a well-known conservation area in the island's north. The park, which is home to a diverse array of native and exotic species, allows visitors to observe Manx wildlife such as the iconic Loaghtan sheep, Manx cats, and various bird species. Stroll through the park's well-kept trails, learn about the island's biodiversity and conservation efforts, and relax in the peaceful natural surroundings. Plan on spending 1-2 hours exploring the Curraghs Wildlife Park.

Finish your day with a scenic drive to the northern tip of the Isle of Man, stopping at the Ayres National Nature Reserve to take in the breathtaking views of the island's rugged coastline and the Irish Sea beyond. As the sun sets below the horizon, enjoy the peaceful solitude and the ever-changing play of light and shadow on the dramatic landscape.

Consider staying in a cozy country cottage or a luxury glamping experience, such as Ballacraine Farm Cottages (from £120 per night) or Knockaloe Beg Farm Glamping Pods (from £150 per night). These distinct lodging options will enable you to seamlessly combine your outdoor adventures with a comfortable and immersive stay.

Spending your fourth day on the Isle of Man's outdoor activities will allow you to fully immerse yourself in the island's natural wonders, from the serene countryside to the rugged coastlines. This day of active exploration will leave you with a deep appreciation for the island's environmental diversity and the Manx people's long-standing connection to the land.

Day 5: Uncovering the Isle of Man's Hidden Gems

On your final day on the Isle of Man, embark on a journey to uncover the island's lesser-known but equally captivating attractions and experiences, ensuring you leave with a well-rounded understanding of this enchanting destination.

Begin the day by visiting the iconic Snaefell Mountain, the island's highest point at 2,036 feet (621 meters) above sea level. Take the Snaefell Mountain Railway, a historic electric railway that will transport you up the mountain's slopes and provide panoramic views of the Manx countryside and the Irish Sea. Enjoy the breathtaking views from the summit while learning about the island's geology and natural history. Plan on spending 1-2 hours exploring the Snaefell Mountain area.

Next, head north to Ramsey, the island's second largest settlement. Stroll through the picturesque harbor, admiring the traditional fishing boats and the town's historic maritime structures. Visit the Manx Transport Museum's satellite location, which houses an intriguing collection of vintage vehicles and motorcycles that have played an important role in the island's transportation history. Spend 1–2 hours exploring Ramsey and the Manx Transport Museum annex.

Explore the island's thriving arts and crafts scene by visiting local galleries, artisan studios, and craft markets. Discover the works of talented Manx artists, potters, weavers, and other skilled artisans who are inspired by the island's natural beauty and cultural heritage. Browse their unique creations, interact with the makers, and consider purchasing a one-of-a-kind souvenir to remember your time on the Isle of Man. Plan to devote 2-3 hours to your arts and crafts exploration.

As the day comes to a close, enjoy a farm-to-table dining experience that highlights the Isle of Man's exceptional local produce and cuisine. Seek out restaurants and eateries that take pride in sourcing their ingredients from the island's vibrant network of small-scale farmers, fishermen, and food producers.

Enjoy the flavors of Manx-reared meats, fresh seafood, artisanal cheeses, and seasonal produce while learning about the island's sustainable food systems and culinary heritage. This dining experience will be an appropriate conclusion to your Manx adventure.

After your final meal, take a leisurely stroll along the Douglas Promenade to reflect on the diverse cultural and natural experiences you've had during your 5-day stay on the Isle of Man. As the sun sets over the Irish Sea, say goodbye to this enchanting island, knowing you've discovered its hidden treasures and immersed yourself in the Manx people's distinct spirit.

Consider booking a room at one of Douglas' elegant hotels or guest houses, such as the Claremont Hotel (from £160 per night) or the Ascot Hotel (from £120 per night). These well-appointed accommodations will provide you with a comfortable and convenient place to end your Isle of Man adventure.

By spending your final day exploring the island's lesser-known but equally captivating attractions, you'll leave with a thorough understanding of the island's cultural, natural, and artistic riches. This carefully curated itinerary will ensure that you make the most of your time on the island, leaving with fond memories and a desire to return.